T0365651

The DEW DROPS....

Akshaya Kumar Das

The DEW DROPS....

An Anthology of *English Poems*...

PARTRIDGE

ISBN:	Softcover	978-1-4828-6904-0
	eBook	978-1-4828-6903-3

Print information available on the last page.

To order additional copies of this book, contact
Partridge India
000 800 10062 62
orders.india@partridgepublishing.com

www.partridgepublishing.com/india

Contents

Sri Akshaya Kumar Das is a budding poet of the present generation. Sri Das was born in village Bharagole under Tirtol P.S.of Dist.Jagatsinghpur of Orissa, India born to Sri Batakrushna Das & Smt.Satyabhama Das on 09th September,1957. His Childhood was spent mostly at the Village studying in Patitapaban UP & ME School.

Sri Das did his Matriculation from Nuabazar High School, Cuttack, Orissa. Sri Das had to face the turbulence of life from youth. Being the 2nd Child to his parents shouldered the responsibilities from the age of 15.A self-made person Sri Das started working at the age of 15. Sri Das presently works as a Manager in a Govt.PSU United India Insurance Co.Ltd.Bhubaneswar, Orissa, India. Completed his graduation from Ravenshaw Evening College & Law Degree from M.S.Law College, Cuttack under Utkal University, Orissa, India. Sri Das has a passion for writing from his college days.

During his college days chosen as the best English Orator of the year in the year 1977.Sri Das has three brothers & three sisters born to his parents. Sri Das is married to Smt.Sangita Pattnaik. Sri Das has two sons named Abhisek & Sashank. Many of his poems were published in a blog created in the rediffiland. com written between the period 2007 to 2010.

Sri Das aspires to complete the noble mission of spending his retired life to writing & specially to English poetry. Some of his English poems are also published internationally recently in the Anthology of Love Poems published by Ardus Publications titled as 'A DIVINE MADNESS" Volume I, V & VI besides regular publications appearing in various Poetic sites of the Facebook. His poems also appear in the ourpoetrycorner@wordpress.com published by Poet Ron DuBour.Sri Das presently resides at

K-5, Kalinga Vihar, Bhubaneswar, Orissa, India

Foreword

A total of 436 poems in the anthology.

The Poems published here belong to all genres. They are on themes of love, Societal issues, current situation prevailing in the world, on nature and on Great personalities to luminaries. Each poem depicts the subjects beautifully In a classy style. The poet has adopted a unique style of writing ending Wonderful finish. The poems on Nature particularly on seasons are Wonderfully described. The seasonal poems have a festive touch in most of Them. The poem touches the psyche of the people at large. The philosophical Poems are superbly penned written in a magnificent style to match beyond the level of expectation of the Poetic Fraternity and readers specially.

With love from the Poet…..

Preface

While writing the preface we have to take a look at the life of the poet which itself Passed through bitter struggles from a very early age. Writing poems has been a Passion since adolescence. From a very young age the poems are written in the His diaries. There was no medium then excepting the Illustrated Weekly which used To publish very few poems besides The Telegraph weekend Magazine. It was Absolutely difficult to find a medium to bring those poems to the limelight.

The inspirations come from a disturbed childhood & a turbulent adolescence of Full of struggle. In most of them an imprint of frustration is beautifully depicted.

But due to a positive attitude towards life the poet has tried to accommodate himself With any given situation that has come in his life without blaming anyone Responsible for the same. Never regretting for what is accomplished or what is not.

The Poet today stands in a fairly better position overcoming the hurdles of time, life & love. The poet was an avid reader of the Time, Life & Fortune Magazine during Youth in the Office library. The poems of Emily Dickinson was the first poem which Affected the poet much "No trust you dear trifling sea". Finally feeling that life Has given everything to him in the form of poetry. Life to him is a beautiful poem.

Struggles are part of life which the poet has overcome fearlessly with a finish.

Before publishing this book the Poet has published many of his works in Facebook.

In fact Facebook gave him the platform to establish himself as a poet of the 21st Century. The accolades from the readers poured in to the take the poet to a fathomless soul searching to realize at a later age that his works have a depth in the content with truth & sublime love. Literature has in fact brought him to International arena. The recognition comes from "The Cost of Existence" Which was published by salisonline.com. A digital webpage followed by his Works being published in Volume I, V & VI of the Anthology of love poems Published by Ardus Publications, Canada with the name "A DIVINE MADNESS".

In fact it is a divine madness that has brought him to the Ocean of Poetries that is Written in this volume. Writing 436 poems in this volume itself. Each poem has a Marvelous input with a marvelous theme which is submitted at the disposal of The readers & fans on whose feedback the Poetical Journey continues to exist.

With love from the Poet..

Dedicated to my Parents, my family, friends, relatives & the Poetic Fraternity whose encouragement & blessings enabled me to accomplish the mission of this book.

2014

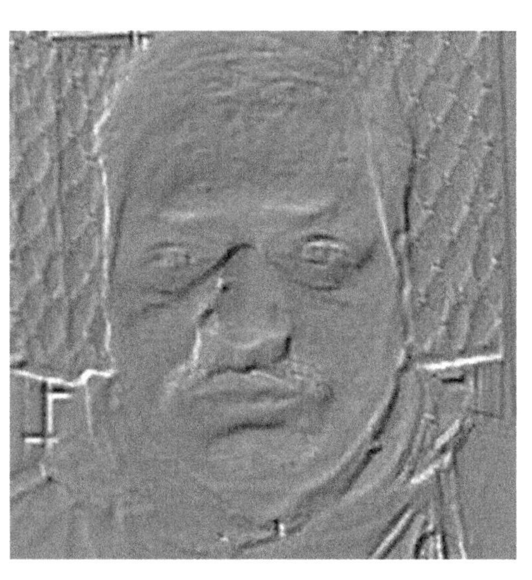

(1)

The Echoes of the deafening voice...

. . . .

Echoes of the voice,
Heard from a deafening silence,
Flickering like a candle in wind.
A flicker of the fire in the grind,
Life halts with the torment.
Pauses for a moment.
Listen to the sighing wind,
That passing like a whiff to find,
Whether the breath
Worth holding in wreathe,
The echoes keep waiting.
It is a thin line in battling
Between life & death.
A thin line of faith,
A thin thread of the trust,
The line of life beseeching the breathe...

. . . .

(2)

Stranded in the Rains...

....

Stranded in the incessant rains,
On the paths the inundated pains,
The ways to traverse,
In composed moods of the verse,
Waiting for the rains to stop,
Drops falling from the sky atop,
The transparent inks of the nature,
Bathing the valley's green amber,
Valley's green amber drenching in the drizzles,
The thirsts of the flora & fauna of the valley in true sizzles,
Stranded souls stripped off their shelter,
Nature's opulent behavior,
Comes raining with the downpour,
The sky opens its sluice gates,
Grins & smiles on the valley's green face

....

(3)

The Youthful Song...

Sing aloud in the closed bathroom.
When the waters from the sprinklers,
Roll down like downpours,
Song after song came humming.
Sang with a full pitch.
Looking at the adolescent girl,
Hanging on the window grills.
Rolling her locks for a windy kiss.
Voices beautifully sang the songs.
Whether somebody listened or not.
It was the entire adolescent gimmick.
That rock the youth.
The sprinklers continued rolling
The waters non-stop.
The song in full volume.
Across the little window grille
The Angel was still hanging.
Songs catches by default.
Pulse by default goes beating.
Beating incessant the drums of youth,
Catch a glimpse of the glance.
Catch a glimpse of the smile.
Bursting into moods of ecstasy in miles.

(4)

The Echoes of Pounding Heart

Seeing you there the heart pounds,
To speak to you words of ecstasy,
The mind travels faster than light,
Just a touch of your hand,
Enough for the soul to take bath.
Take a happy nap.
Making the moods.
Dance in exaltation.
Life seems to have accomplished.
Time seems to be running away.
Even trying to hold it in palm.
Tides recede back so fast.
Still the heart pounds.
Accidental meeting on the crossroads.
The wings of the soul readying for a flight to her,

For a soulful embrace.
For soulful happiness,

(5)

Death

. . . .

Death snatches away people untimely.
Why death snatches away people untimely?
Ask the question for an Answer,
When you ask self too,
The self silently evades the answer,
No answer to these questions,
Life is too short & uncertain here,
Left behind mute spectators,
Remember it for the time,
The gravity of woe immeasurable,
During the happening,
Acclimatize the self to the situation,
The bare truth,
Death will visit one day all of us,
Only time,
The moment not known.
Short lived one's leave an imprint in the mind,
Thinking why it happens so?
The harsh truth of life,
Predicament in rife.
Once born,
Death too is born.

. . . .

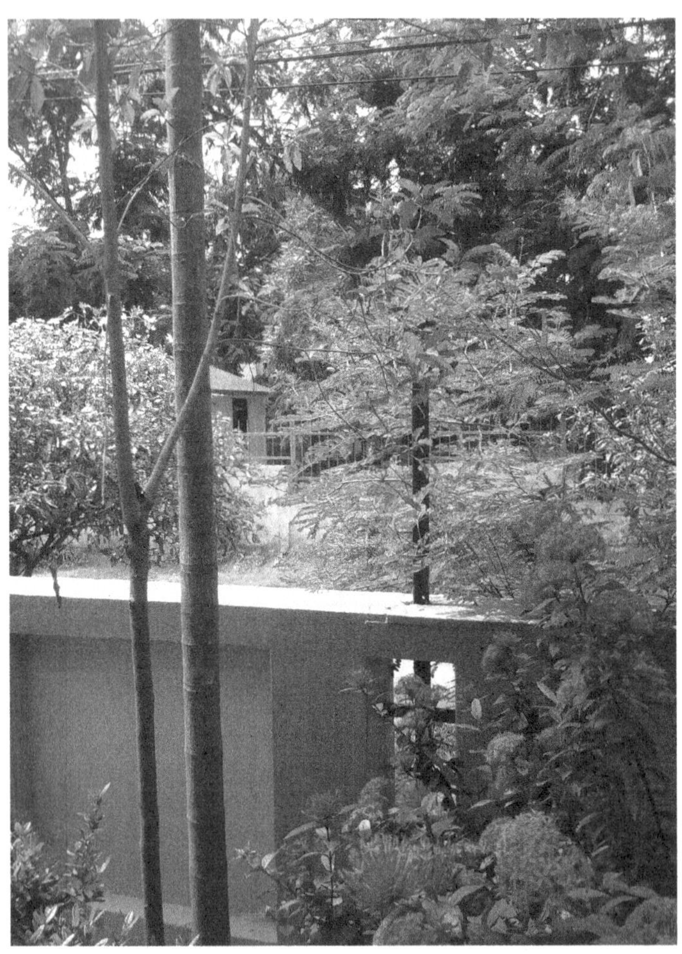

(6)

The Garden in Greenery,

. . . .

Pregnant with flowers,
From a distance a small cottage,
Looks at the morning walker,
Walk in the yards,
Shed your sweats,
Weights and thoughts,
Beauty mesmerizes the soul,
Drink the beauty to the lees,
Am not Ulysses or Cinderella to please,
I am Nature,
My job is to Nurture.
Nurture your passion,
Nurture your dreams.
See them accomplish,
With breeze of freshness.

. . . .

(7)

Salute to the Army..

....

The Rescuers were noble souls,
Rescuing the million people,
That had gone afloat,
When the boat of life sinks,
At nature's wink.
Everything go berserk.
wails & cries,
Save our souls,
All start ringing the pulse.
Charity comes from the military.
The fury of the ferocious nature.
The valleys & the domes sinking.
To the abyss of Death.
The abysmal bed,
From where none rises,
The rescuers arrive in camouflage,
Food, water & shelter the trinity to regain.
Hope against hope,
When the nectar of life starts spilling,
In sheer chill,

A distant howling, far away cry...
Water....water...water everywhere...
But not a drop to drink...
Charity starts its job.
Just a befitting Grand Salute in the soul,
Comes from the spontaneous soul...
Oh! Army.
A standing ovation to your soldiers,
Risking own life you give your shoulders

....

(8)

The Bud Hood....

....

The petals in buds enclosure,
Embracing the fold with each other,
As the sun beams splash their presence,
The petals slowly opening their faces.
A honey bee from nowhere arrives,
Spreading its wings on the fathomless pollens.
With its little fangs, wings & stings.
Message of classic nature love
The neighboring flower in trove,
With swift breeze the flowers dances,
Nodding in solitude rejoicing the grace,
Spray the perfumes of fragrance.
The fragrant perfumes of the saintly flower.
Embrace the pollen into adore,
For the seed to mature,
The ignoble ways of nature,
Leaves an imprint on time of it's beautiful grace.
Compelling the soul to alight in transcendence.
The bud hood comes to an end,
Leaving the fruits of its labour on the earth's bed...

....

(9)

The Asylum owners...

....

Life is an asylum,
A road from birth till death.
Life an eternal asylum,
A miniature replica of the mass universe.
For a moment try to catch life.
From the mother's womb till the funeral pyre.
A journey full of stories and satire.
Love it,
Hate it.
Eat it,
Destroy it.
The invisible destiny
Holding the reigns of life
The mercy reigning over time.
Childhood in the mother's lap.
Youth in the beloved's arms.
Old age at the mercy's door,
All along imprisoned without a wish.
Imprisoned like a beautiful chicken,

Buttered & battered to be butchered.
The soul in your ignorance,
Faces the guillotines countless sharp razors.
In helpless state Do or die.
The beautiful life always pronounced,
A merciless sentence of death at the end.

. . . .

(10)

On the Crossroads...

An eternal earth,
An ephemeral birth,
Earth waits till eternity,
Since time immemorial.
Millions come & gone,
But the earth still on.
Life is temporary,
The earth permanent.
Breathe & survive till death,
Life confined to time.
Once consumed,
All expire.
All merge to the earth.
The mother absorbs all in its broad chest,
In a temporary world eternal dreams,
The moment life gone soul screams,
Body melts & mingles into the earth's vapor in realms,
The soul captures another body,
Another frame in re-birth.
The invisible soul lives oblivious.

(11)

The Last Look....

. . . .

From the glass cube,
life of my beloved.
Gasping for a comeback.
Passes waving bye...
Outside the glass cube,
The last touch of her.
Abhor,
A Wreath on the lifeless body.
A fresh rose bud in memoriam.
Unable to touch her lifeless body.
Place wreath on the coffin fully draped.
Sleeping in deep sleep She....
In deep sojourn.
Sobbing eyes touching her.
In all transparency visible but lifeless.
With her last look of love & smile of grace.

. . . .

(12)

Struggle for Survival

The struggle for survival does not end.
Birth till death maintain the trend,
The struggle for food,
For shelter,
For love,
For space.
Continues ....till the last breathe.
In this fragile world so much struggle.
Walk, run. Walk ...run..
Had it been known,
Would have preferred not to be born.
Being born then the struggle.
Struggle to save the self.
Always act in passion,
Lest you fail to reason.
A chain that always pulls you down.
Success may be at hand,
But one slip puts you back at zero.
The level zero difficult to start,
No gimmick in looking back.
Just by hook or crook be there.
Climb the ladders step by step…

(13)

Autumn comes knocking...

....

Autumn arrives with a knock,
On the day of vernal equinox,
When the equator exactly,
In the middle of the earth's axis,
The day equals the night.
A feeling of equanimity comes.
The festive moods catching up.
From tomorrow the sun will be north bound.
The weather will sing pleasantries.
In eastern India the festival season catches up mood.
Maa Durga will arrive on the earth.
Killing the demon Mahisasura for his evil nature,
Winning the war for truth to prevail over the evil,
A Replica of woman's right to prevail on the Universe.
Granting boons to women to excel over men.
A Great season arrives
The destruction of the ten headed demon... "Ravan"
A Great Oath taken.

To preserve the dignity of women on earth.
Celebrations remind mankind to
perform his truthful duties.
To preserve the mother earth,
Mother Nature,
Give each woman her due share of life.
Give each mother her due place of worship.

....

(In October Indians celebrate Durga Puja a very important Hindu Festival. Particularly Eastern India is famous for the religious tone added to the festival. Durga Puja i.e., Worshipping Mother Durga an ikon of woman power killing the Demon Mahisasura for his notoriety. Mahisasura was demon who was a very powerful giant who wrought havoc by his rule. The God's from heaven were his main target. The Demon was jealous of the God's ruling the universe and their stay in heaven. But because of his enormous power acquired through his prayers, He wanted his supremacy to be there in the planet. His ego was the main culprit of his ambitious self. Goddess Durga killed the demon through her tantrums of beauty and angelic looks to which Mahisasura was attracted. In the war Mahisasura fell to the Goddess and was killed by her. Huge Effigies of Ravan the Demon is also burn in many places across India.)

(14)

The Nine Nights of Navaratri....

....

The nine night of Navaratri,
The nine different incarnations of the mother,
Celebrations begin from East to West of India.
South to North of India.
Indians celebrate the occasion with tempo.
Idol warship of the Goddess Durga
Burn the effigy of the Demon Ravan
prevailing Truth over the evil,
Truth alone triumphs echoing in the air,
The Nine Nights fasting ending with a fair,
Gujratis in India play Garba Dance in full swing.
Whole Nights go in dance & songs with musical choirs,
Young to old, poor to rich everyone on the musical chair,
Festive moods to fasting modes,
Dreams come true with the autumnal nodes,
Peace & Prosperity touching every step of life
Good over evil will win the ambience in rife,

New wears, cakes & pastries to chocolates
Soft to cold flows abundant with
atmosphere with accolades,
The celebrities to the commoner
everyone in moods of rejoice,
The poor to the destitute celebrate with their own means,
Never envying the neighbor how little be their demeanor,
Happy Nights of nine for everyone in divine tempers,
Each & every soul relishing in fun & fair,
A wish in every soul let the universe breathe peace,
A wish in every soul let the universe breathe prosperity,
A wish in every soul let the universe breath happiness.

....

(15)

Sculptor's Dreams...

....

The Nude Sculpting...
The Nudeness cast on stone images,
Beautifully engraved on the stone images trail,
Awesome cravings engraved with the sharp augurs nails,
The soul of the sculptor embossed in the Art.
The soul of the sculptor engraved with the heart.
The Art of love making in the edifice of sculptor,
Miniature Nude Postures crafted on
the wheels with picture,
Sexiest appeal to the eyes of the viewer,
Sexist depictions engraved with graphic images,
The legendary monument written on the granite block,
Standing silent since time immemorial
as time's mute witness,
In the lifeless stone pieces life infused.
Love in fusion of rainbows dreaming,
The art of nude sculpting by the
sculptor's artistic supremacy,
Nude couples making love since
ages in absolute intimacy...

The eyes just remain on hold imagining the supermanship,
Love played the theme of life with the
stone images of the anchored ship,
The passionate souls in union
embracing passionate dreams,
Creating fusion of the devouring minds of a voyeur,
Love knows no barriers,
Love knew no places,
No colors or religion...
The artistic pin-pointed carvings on the carved stone,
The mind weaved such beautiful conceptual imageries,
The mesmerism of the captive pursuits
shelved in the space's treasuries,
Excelled for ages the superman's skilled artefacts,
Paying a penance to the posterity to relook into the facts...

....

(16)

Golden Silence...

. . . .

Volume of silence.
Stood fathomless,
With years gone in between,
Memories still hunt the siren,
In the shadows of moods,
Figure out the solitude of the woods,
Standing there,
Waiting there,
Anger baiting,
Hurled glances.
Still catapulted.
Feelings of time.
That life was a rhyme.
Despite opposition from within,
Still make it somehow to happen,
Still a beat within,
keeps beating in vein..
The fenced world's prison,
The prison giving only pain,
Succumb to the injuries
The wounds of the centuries,
Life gives nothing but pains of centuries...

. . . .

(17)

The Gothic tales....

....

Gothic tales of Greek mythology,
Beautifully replicated...
Slavery & torture,
Even the lion spares the slave,
As it was its master of one time.
Seeing the master inside the dungeon.
But humans fail...
The cruel hands of destiny
Putting the slaves into gaol,
Under the tortuous labor,
Imprisonment,
Slash beaten,
Visible imprints over the body blown up,
Blood baths inhuman treatment Show up,
Man over man,
Ruler over the slaves.
That was history,
Spoke of saga of the slavery.
Slaves handcuffed & chained.
Man is born free but everywhere in chains.

Put inside the small cage made for wild Lions.
The tears drops rolled down from the wells of sorrow.
Is this the world God dreamed of...?
Made one man to suffer at the hands of the other,
Drawing a huge line between man & man,
Satires whistling at the tortuous ordeal of man.
Sadists on throne.
Enjoying the power shows of ignorance in feign....

....

(18)

The Ladder of Life....

....

The ladder,
That life is,
Each step carries the load,
The load of life,
But one simple mistake,
One wink of the eye,
If life slips,
Gasp.,
End in death,
The lost chapter,
From birth till death,
Keep crawling,
Walking,
Running,
Till the last breathe,
Stops abruptly ending,
When the ladder falls,
A meteor falls,
The pulse fails,
Tears jerk up.
All the bubbles vanish,
With a wink of eye in finish,

....

(19)

A Dormant Volcano

A dormant volcano sleeps,
But wakes up at times from the sleep,
Every man for that sake,
Is a poet
With dormancy captivating him.
When the volcano erupts,
The lava,
With its poetic curves,
Spread like a serpent,
In the surrounding,
Where it is situated,
A poet when erupt,
Will erupt the lava of poetry
Which affects?
The heart, love, life & time,
Mind is never barren,
The boon to create,
Human wishes to bear fruit,
Only it needs a touch,
Needs little pricking at times,
A Genius sleeps inside with whim,

(20)

The Blind Imaging..

....

The Blind Images rolls in the cradle of time,
Within the closed eyes rocking with a rhyme,
In the deeper fathoms of the sea,
Under the oceans seven layers,
Dreams were rolling in folders,
Cascading into the cliffs of the thought,
Imagining & Imaging within the closed port,
The molten process of thought,
Trying to catch a glimpse of the dreams dream,

....

(21)

The Soul's Vision

. . . .

The soul was flying into the oblivion,
The cliff was moisten,
Full of clouds & moist droplets of rain,
Glistening with the shining sun.
The soul afloat in a dream with fun,
Sailing through the dark waters.
Bottled into a cocoon's shelter,
Waiting for a blast of the bubbles.
The unknown palpitations in feeble,
Beatings across the heart in treble,
Going unheard like rolling rubble,
Reflecting mirrors of memories,
Lost in oblivion in the visions treasuries,

. . . .

(22)

The Nature's Groves

The shelters of nature
Weaved for the feathers,
They weaved such a huge shelter
Built of nature's fiber.
The onlooker feels baffled at the wonder,
The mystery behind the designs décor,
The décor of divine attire,
The world of his dreams the passionate weaver,
Built with such touch of the beak,
What a wonderful finish & make...

(23)

The Dream Merchants

Tearing the tides of the ocean's heart,
The mermaid arrived,
Half woman
Half Fish,
The eyes wondering,
The sighs of echoes of the mermaids,
Beautiful fairy maidens from the ocean,
Serpentine linings with dreams of heaven,
Ah! For a moment the onlooker in catch,
Mesmerism of the sea in the stretch,
If the mermaid could alight in my den.
Life's fortune in hand to just feign,
Nothing more nothing less than heaven...

(24)

Poetic Mermaid...

....

In the ocean of the poet's thoughts.
Poetry is a beautiful mermaid in the pot,
The poet when jots the lines.
Lives in a world of illusion,
Thoughts that flood in the corner of the winks get born.
With each tide that came ashore,
A thought recedes back from the fathomless shore,
For the mermaid's hunt.
When the seed sprouts,
The embryo silently conceived,
The pregnant poet eschews feeling relieved,
Nurtures & loves the umbilical connection,
With the language in true emotion,

....

(25)

Standing on the cliff of life...

Standing on the verge of the cliff,
She closed her eyes,
For the final fall,
The heart was crying,
Tears flowing like a river,
Betrayed by lover...
She was shaken by the act.
Two lives before the suicide squad.
The one who never saw life from the womb,
The unwed mother's decision from the tomb,
She can't move with the pregnant frame.
Rejected, abused she stood.
There on the verge of the cliff.
In virtual moods of jumping in a whiff,
The fetus was too shattered.
Making emphatic calls
To save the mother.

Sending telepathic signals,
Through the veins,
Through the placental connect,
Don't end.
Don't end.
The fetus calling in frantic pain,
Dissuading the negative mind.
Oh! Mom please be kind,
Let me see the light.
Will stand by your side.
Dedicate life for you in your stride,
Set on track your devastated life.
O Mom...Stay back...Stay Back life.

....

(26)

Cry the beloved

Cry the beloved for you,
My heart bleeds for you,
With your departure from life,
Could not stop it.
Gasping for life,
Slowly losing myself into the abysmal.
In my self-annihilation,
Invading my soul,
Pierced into pieces,
Breaking each memory,
That bore the mark of relation.
Built in the Empire of love.
Time only was laughing at my misfortune.
Life mocking existence.
Feeling as if I do not deserve life.
Prefer a bloody death.
Cannot leave a last wish for you.
Fearing the world would never forgive you,
Forgiving.
Freeing you from the clutches,
My love.
Platonic for me.
An unconditional affair.

(27)
The Eternal Betrayal

....

The eye is the great betrayer,
What we see one moment,
Does not appear next,
Like a mirage,
We hunt for the image,
That disappeared,
With one wink,
Went out of sight.
Only the image,
Gets imprinted in the mind,
Regret life long,
Regret & wonder,
If at all,
There was such an image,
Cursing the self,
A feeling to console,

My questioning mind,
Such things,
Like a falling star,
Difficult to catch.
The mandrake root,
Gives immortality,
So difficult to find.
Consult my Guru,
My soul for an answer,
In silence.
In deep meditations.
If the image could reappear.
Believe, believe my eyes.

. . . .

(28)

The Boatman's Journey...

The Boatman's journey.
With the oar in hand,
The boatman does not care,
Relish in heart,
Sailing the boat,
His moods visit into,
The soul of the nature,
To find if the boat would,
Carry him ashore,
Carry him to shore,
For a beautiful gold fish
To feed the hunger,
Of his appetite,
His life with the nature,
Is a gift of god?
His job ferrying,
The traveler from this side of the shore,
To the other side.
River his life,
Air his energy,
Oar the life support.
On the huge water body,
Imagines & eking out a living.

(29)

The Unique Truth of Existence

....

One moon,
One sun,
One earth,
One life,
All are one,
What an irony,
When all the three,
Moon, Sun & Earth are eternal,
Life is temporary.
But the other side of life,
When you watch it's multitudes.
Every moment millions are born,
Every moment millions gone.
The predicament of life.
It is not one like the moon, the sun or the earth.
A wise man only counts the ordeal in his own way.
Ponders over the mystery.
The story of inner truth,
Probably never knows the outer earth.
To the spheres that exist beyond.

....

(30)

The Understanding fails...

When the understanding fails,
Everything fails,
Everything collapses,
The sky starts falling,
Crashing comes the world,
Trying to assimilate the splinters,
Again does not help,
Difficult to reunite
The soul from the splinters...

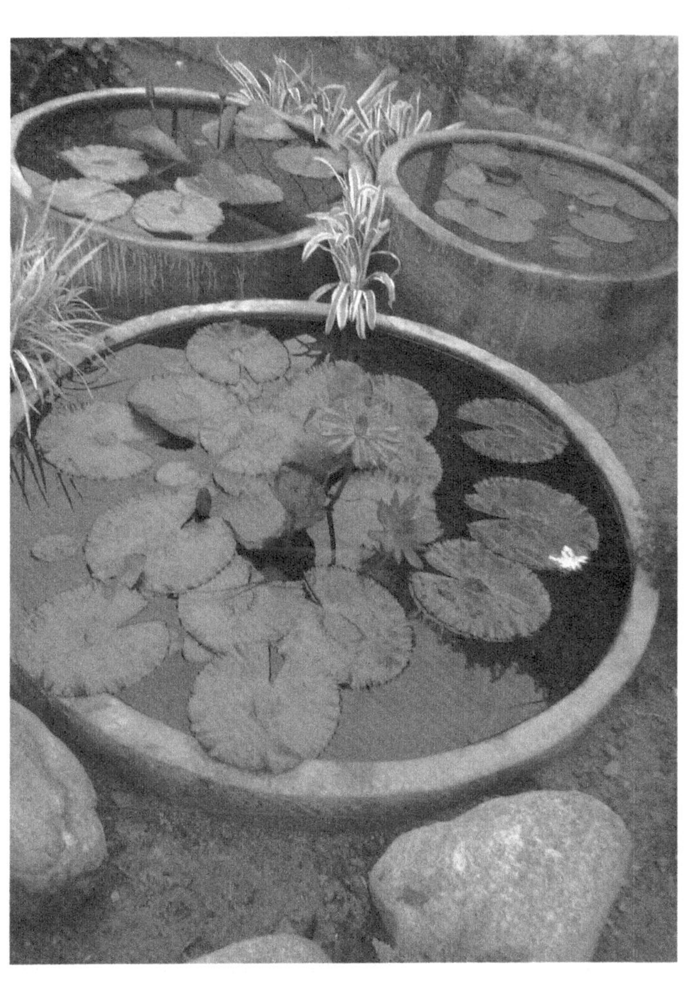

(31)

Dew on Lotus...

Pearls of dew drops,
Dew drops gliding on the lotus,
In the waters of the pond,
The gliding dew drops,
On the surface of the leaves,
Like drops of mercury,
Shine on the leaf,
When wind blows,
Drop the floating bulb,
Into the fathomless bed beneath,
The lotus buds start blooming,
With the visiting rays of the dawn,
The shining petals in white & pink,
Attire walk ramp,
On the surface of the pond,
The eyes blink at them,
Heaving at the beauty,
Awesome feelings inside,
The pearl feel infatuated,
Assemble the pearl drops,
Into a garland,
In speechless silence.

(32)

Taking a Nap...

The shore's swelling tides,
Washing the feet of the ocean,
The recurring tides,
Why they run to the shore?
As if they have nowhere to run.
Running towards the shore,
One above the other,
With dazzling bubbles sprinkling over,
The eyes taking a nap,
Jumping high with each visiting tide,
Sitting on the fence,
Swimming with the tide,
The weekend visitors,
Attracted to the shore,
Age not a barrier,
Young to old everyone,
Take nap,
Refreshing the piles of junk,
Accumulated in the psyche's trunk...

(33)

The Obsession...

....

When my soul has fallen in love with you,
Have to hear the frantic calls.
The telepathic calls,
That comes in invisible waves.
Is such attached to the invisible waves?
Often get the calls,
An emerging feeling in the heart,
Urging me to talk to you,
In my silence,
In my solitudes,
Keep talking to you.
It is for you I exist.
It is for you I am dying.

....

(34)

The River is flowing...

The river of poem,
Flows by my mind's village.
Since time immemorial it has been flowing,
As I get into the depth of the river,
The river catches me with its currents,
Traps me,
Drags me underneath,
To its fathomless bed,
As I swim into the depth,
Feel breathless with false promises,
With uncertain fears,
Try to pull out myself,
Difficult to pull out.
Just sleep into silence.
Sink there.
Penning down the betrayal,
From the river's drowning water.

(35)

Life...

Life has a dawn,
When dawn is born,
The dawn begins to bloom,
Slowly the closed petals form,
Planted by the leaving night.
Life has a morning in wait,
Morning the infant,
The flower starts opening in fancy,
The petals slowly open their lips,
With the arrival of the rays just sip,
Life has a noon,
Noon the prime of youth in boon,
In the prime of youth,
The eyes start winking at truth,
At every damsel in absolute faith,
With wild attractions & lust.
Life has an afternoon,
Afternoon the adulthood in reign,
In adulthood life a ferocious lion,
Full of energy brimming to burn,
Life has a dusk.

Dusk with the setting sun at the horizon,
Where life changes to evening,
Life has an evening,
Evening with the constellation of stars,
Life has a night amidst wild roars,
In the night the North Star shines,
Amidst the constellations of stars,
Night ending with the dawn's innocence,
End is the transfer of legacy.
Life surrounded by different stages.
In a day itself,
In a night itself,
With days chasing nights,
Chasing life.
In between life's varied stages,
Roles altered by time.
Playing the tunes to the gimmick of life,

....

(36)

The Threads of relationship...

If she is not well,
How can I be well?
If she is not happy,
How can I be happy?
If she is crying,
I am crying.
If she laughs,
Have to laugh.
If she smiles,
Have to smile.
If she is in heaven,
Have to be in heaven.
The She life,
Am He.
Caught between
Threads of She & He.

(37)

The Soul Connect...

. . . .

It is a soul connect,
When the soul is connected,
Forget my darling,
Wherever you stay,
Will connect with you.
It is a soul connect.
Difficult to disconnect.
An invisible thread binding us.
Faster than light.
In moments I am with you,
A poet knows his lovers.
Better than anyone,
His waiting at the gates,
Compliments,
Only in words his sails,
Only in words his life.
The glass of his soul shines,
In all transparency.

. . . .

(38)

Vying for a touch

Vying for a touch,
The oar of the boatman,
That ferries,
From one end of the river,
To the other.
Between the sails,
Sailing across,
At times,
Loosing contact with the ground,
In the depth of the waters,
The boat sails,
The oar the only support,
With the beloved,
Perched on one end,
The boatman balancing,
The boat ashore,
With the moonstruck beloved,
Bathing in moon lit night,
Sizzling sensuous appeals,
The roaring bodies groaning,
The flames dying.
The ripe passions,
Vying for a touch of trance.

(39)

The Songs of Repentance...

If love was a crime,
We committed it,
Remember the lamp post,
Where you stood,
Helplessly watching my mood,
The assassination,
Tears silently rolled their way,
Explaining the heart's saga of separation.
The rebukes hurled,
Questioning the innocent affair,
Like a rock you stood in grave silence,
In mute tolerance,
Your tears muted me to silence,
My fears were finding their freedom,
Let the assassin commit the ransom,
Let blood spill over hacking us to death,
Let another chapter Romeo & Juliet,

Heer Ranjha story be written,
Happily laugh at the assassins,
Let them kill satiate their appetite.
The merciless act of the brutal mayhem,
Helplessly watching the shackles,
Locked from tip to toe.
Each other's brutal separation,
Brutal assassination,
If love was our crime,
We committed it.
Lest how many times you kill us,
Hang us put us into the gallows,
Nothing can separate us.
Love is immortal,
Even if the ending is so fatal.

....

(40)

The Incorrigible Nature.

....

Peeping into your secrets,
My eyes were blushing,
My eyes were drinking,
Mesmerism of the untapped valleys,
Resting the head,
Between the thin line of the cleavage,
Stood the innocent hillock,
Fallen asleep.
Roaming in the lagoon,
Bathing in the water fall,
The topless hills.
No one knew the source of the water.
Falling since time immemorial,
Countless lovers bathed there.
Capturing the sizzling,
Hot moods symbolic acts of cupidity.
The tourist to the thinker,
Who ever knew the secret?
Engrossed with the scenic cascade,
Bathing freedom of youth,
Drinking the nectars of the cascades,
Falling from nature.

The lovers baring their hearts there.
An unique signature in graphic attire.
With accidentally bitten,
Tongues innocently swallowing the moment.
Lips swallowing the love bitten birds,
From hugs to passionate dreams,
Engraving the stories in realms,
On the soft cheeks,
A shining droplet,
Missile of the arrow,
Piercing into the soul of the lovers,
With the passionate feelings,
With wound marks,
Leaving the marks to unravel,
The stories engraving cupidity in marvel,

....

(41)

The Innocent Pebbles...

. . . .

The pebbles waiting for a touch of my feet,
The water flowing beneath comes from the stream,
The pebbles always wash themselves,
Roll a little rock a little,
Sing rhymes with the gargles of the flowing water,
While walking on the stretch of the pebbles,
The feet get the pricks & the pinches,
Relaxing the palpitations from the racing pulse
Rubbing the toes with punches & needle pricks,
Energy flows through muscles giving a soothing feel.
Love the pebbles for their touch.

. . . .

(42)

The Shadows of Death...

The shadow of life,
Always moves after life,
A Ghost,
Chasing minutely,
Every action,
To reaction.
A vacuum of existence,
Beyond the aura of the life,
Every step you move,
Every step you climb,
Every look you throw,
There is a cause,
There is an effect,
That touches & vanishes.
At times life wonders,
At the Ghosts,
At the Shadows,
If at all they existed.
Trying to unravel the enigma of life,
What happens after life?

When the breathing stops,
What happens beyond?
Questions always,
Now & then,
Baffle,
In the mental pastures.
Failing attempts
To touch the shadows,
To touch the ghosts,
Discover the truth,
The reason of the shadows,
The Ghosts.

. . . .

(43)

The First shock of Life..

....

The first shock of life comes from you,
You who promised to hold my hands for ever,
You who assured me your hand for life,
Volunteered to be support for life,
Did not hesitate a moment,
To leave me half way through,
Never thought a moment,
Leaving me to suffer the mutiny.
Never looked back at the loss of destiny,
Lying there in the middle of the road,
My platonic frame was lying there,
Waiting for a glimpse,
It pains to see you pass in silence,
Ignoring our meeting points,
Even crossed the roads you preferred to distance.
The insurmountable pain keeps piling up on existence.
Do not know for how long have to suffer the stance.
Question the purpose of existence.

....

(44)

A Long Breathe..

. . . .

Take a long breathe,
Death comes laughing,
At the end of life,
From the time of birth,
Till the time of death,
The breath keeps happening,
The game of breathing in & out,
To breathe is life,
To breathe out is death,
Events after events,
Happening,
But death never bothers man,
Even though it followed in disguise,
Where ever man visited,
From temple to church to mosques,
Everywhere death followed life.
The two sides of one coin,
The opposite of life is death.
Once the breathing stops,
Panic for little air.
Man gasps for life.
To elope from the clutches of death.
Life from the claws of death,

. . . .

(45)

War & Peace...

....

The havocs that wars write,
Live the warring community in fright,
Destroying the peace of mind,
Destroying the homes to grind,
The worst sufferer,
The innocent children & women,
The victims of the war,
The war leaves scars of life time,
Difficult to heal,
The worst comes from the shadow attacks,
The camouflage cracks,
Destroying the enemy camps,
Writing havoc,
Watch the war as a mute spectator,
Helpless situations.
Praying for the war to stop,
Life please comes to normalcy.
Peace to comeback leaving complacency,
The wounds wrought by the war to heal,
God give civic sense to the warring communities,
God is one why fight wars?

Sad truth,
Sad realities on deserted roads,
From ancient times wars have been human passion,
From time to time humans to fight for supremacy.
Fight for revenge,
Fight for territory.
Fight for blood,
Fight for rivers,
Fight against each other,
At times for nothing,
Fanatic ideologies,
When life,
Such an ephemeral affair,
So temporary why fight wars,

. . . .

(46)

Bare the Heart...

Just bare open the heart,
Bare the soul,
The Soul's blank horizon,
When in distress,
Open the closed box of the mind,
Before the water falls,
Speak aloud to the nature,
Sing aloud to the nature,
The echoes of the nature will recoil back.
Feel the vibrations of the echoes.
Echoes of the nature's message,
Remove the blockade that blocks the mind.
Remove the shackles that bind.
Once opening the petals of soul,
The petals will sing the song to lull,
Song of Peace,
The gravity of the woes vanish,
Freedom just unleash,
From the bondages of the moment,
Bondages of the times inclement,
Remember the born freedom.

Never shackle the self in the chained dome,
For much of your pain is self-chosen.
Discontinue to suffer for your choices often,
The wrong option,
Just stop being choosy.
The true meaning of the life's sauce.
Sing the voice of Peace.

. . . .

(47)

The Village School...

The Village School...
Just five yards away,
Stood the village school,
The primary school,
As a ritualistic infant,
Visit the school,
Every morning,
With
Bag full of books,
Attend the classes,
one after one,
one by one,
Failure to answer the questions,
Teacher's rebuke to familiar canes.
Arithmetic to Nursery Rhymes,
Little black slate with a piece of chalk,
A daily prayer for the welfare of the being,
For the welfare of the society,
The country,
Followed the classes,
The bells rang at hourly intervals.
From one to ten,
Ten to hundred,

A for Apple,
Z for Zebra...
From A to Z all alphabets followed,
The menu one after the other,
The slates in the class room,
competed with each other in absolute mom,
For a check by the teacher,
The teacher slapped or caned,
For the wrong answers,
Followed the rhymes,
Jack & Jill went up the hill,
Jack fell down & broke his crown,
Jim came tumbling after,
Rehearsing another,
Twinkle Twinkle little star,
How I wonder what you are,
The Recreation break,
A Half an hour break,
The midday meal hour,
Rush home for half an hour,
Run for the afternoon session.
Hangovers douse the session,
Everyone including the teacher feeling drowsy,
The after meals drowsiness douse,
The games period really amazing,

Teams were always set against each other,
One won and the other lost,
As the school bell rang,
Our ecstasies just sprang,
Run for home.
The cowboys home bound with the herd,
Before the sun started setting in the west end,
Forgot to remember the chapter of the school,
A lantern lighted with the evening prayer,
Homework followed the usual affair,

....

(48)

After the Before...

. . . .

Before ...before...
Before you ....read...
Check...before you check...
Touch...before you touch...
Hug...before you hug...
Imagine...before you imagine...
Love....before you love...
Feel....before you feel...
Beseech...before you beseech...
Pray...before you pray...
Die....before you die...
Live...before you live...
Commit...before you commit.
Sin...before you sin...
Atone...before you atone...
Forgive...before you forgive...
Leave...leave...leave...

. . . .

(49)

The Tranquil Dawn...

....

Tranquil dawn,
Chills of the winter,
Lots of dew drops sitting on the grass.
A sober atmosphere,
Morning walker's walking barefoot,
On the grass,
To massage the feet with the dew,
The grass smiling with the dew's radiance,
Never crying with pain for the trampling,
God's own country the grass does not feel small,
Prides at its meaningful existence.
Something to be given,
Something to be sacrificed,
When you give,
Give it with an open heart,
When you sacrifice,
Sacrifice with an open heart,
Charity must begin at home,
Charity must dawn,
Start from the beginning.

....

(50)

The False Glory...

....

The False Chasing...
Run after glory,
Run after fame,
Like a thief you run,
To snatch the rewards,
From the time's blank space,
Time's blind walls,
Hang them on the walls,
Show them to everyone,
What you got in your life time,
What you may get posthumously,
Waits with patience,
Everyday every minute,
A mad chase,
With a mad ambition,
In the back yard of mind,
Man runs,
No one chases him,
No one pursues him,
No one stops him,
Neither his competitors nor his benefactors,
But he himself chasing himself,
His own emotions,
His very own thoughts,
Puts him on the race course.

What a sad irony.
Trying to be something,
Someone,
Everyone here runs for a name,
Everyone here runs for little fame,
Poor to rich everyone wants a name,
Without realizing for a moment,
Life's goals are all false,
Life came from the dusts,
Will perish into the dusts...
But still the chasing does not stop
For a moment till the last breathe.

....

(51)

Birth till Death a Beautiful Chase.

. . . .

The Great insight,
Knowing things well keep chasing,
That's probably a wish flows in our blood,
From the moment our birth.
Look when you were born,
Your very cry was a chase,
Symbolizing the enigma of life,
That waits ahead,
One has to run towards the goal,
The very goal starts with first breathe,
Ends with the last breathe.
In a mundanely existence,
The commands of the Omni powerful,
Preordained,
Who invisibly watches every action of yours?
Civilizations will come & go,
Relics remain,
Past, present & future always tense,
Grammar of Life,
Generations to continue their sojourn,
For the great insight.
The inner truths, meaning & pursuit.

. . . .

(52)

The Secret Truths...

....

The sphere has a hole,
The black hole,
While one attracts matter,
The other astronomical ether,
Truths never known,
Wherever there is hole,
The purpose of hole,
Animals to humans have nine holes,
To keep the pulse beating,
Each hole has distinct role,
The burrow is a hole,
Dug by the animal,
Ants to centipedes,
Love to reside there,
It is man who constructs,
A house of squares,
Of mud walls to live in,
With thatched roof tops,
To live with Mother Nature,
The hidden truth of the hole,
Is an amazing story,
Amazing history,
Amazing poetry for life.

....

(53)

The Orphans of Destiny.

....

Caught in the Sewerage,
The fire raging in the mind,
The truths when comes to light.
The world will never know,
Who the father of the baby is?
The baby that was dumped in the sewers,
Now fights a battle of legacy,
Battle for Paternity.
The Mother to save her virginity,
Dumped the baby in the sewerage.
By an accidental turn of events,
The test of paternity proves you,
You are guilty,
Guilty acts of youthful exuberance,
Fanatic love affair,
The empire that you struggled to build,
Now belongs to him,
The lifelong hatreds,
The lifelong neglects,
That he suffered,
Belonged to none but you.
Give him his due shares,
Give him the paternity he fights for,

....

(54)

The Ancient Life...

....

The ancient man lived
In caves,
Lived in jungles,
Lived on tree tops,
Lived in forests,
Lived near rivers,
Lived nude,
In all nudity,
Everything was open,
From agriculture,
To child rearing,
Huge patch of barren land,
Cultivated by him,
Crops to children all flourished,
Abundantly with nature,
With leaves as the covers,
Ate bare fruits,
Leaves of the trees,
Vegetables of the forest,
Drank waters from the streams,
Bathed in the gorges,
In the water falls,
Hide him secured in the caves.

....

(55)

Stone Age Rhymes...

....

The Stone Age Rhymes,
The stones when rubbed,
Produce fire,
Man learned the art of firing,
From stones produced,
Artillery to face the wild animals,
Then used the same against each other,
Became the headman of the herd,
The head Patriarch,
As the civilization flourished,
Man learnt the use of metals,
From metals produced artillery,
For safety from wild animals,
Then from the tribes,
Trespassing into their geography.
Drank the blood of the wild animals after the hunt,
Did not know what to do,

With the blood that flowed after the kill.
Slowly learnt to use the tongue,
Drank the blood after the kill,
The meat of the animal too.
Learnt slowly to set fire,
Boil water for cooking.
Mastered the art of Cooking,
Shifted from place to place for hunting.
Mastering the art of surviving,
With the wild animals & innocent plant dome,
....

(56)

The Dry Leaves..

....

The Dry leaves..
Drops when dry,
Keep dropping to the ground,
The ground loves them,
Falling on its nude body,
Covering the bare earth,
With its countless leaves,
When you trample them,
No hiss.
The sole of your feet,
Slips on them,
Lot of dry leaves,
Amassing in the backyard.
Like a painter's brush,
Dry Leaves paint a huge spread,

....

(57)

Winter's Arrival..

....

The winter has arrived,
The winter is a child,
In my backyard,
The dews too blush,
With their shining faces.
The dew sits on the grass.
The whole night's incessant droppings.
From the heaven,
As if the heaven dropped the dews to bath the grass,
The grass waited such long,
For a dew bath,
The soil looks soaked,
The drops on the lotus leaves,
Looks like a small mass on the leaves,
Radiant beams soaking them,
Like a thirsty traveler in a desert,
Logs of wood put on fire,
A campfire takes place,
With children, men & women,
Surrounding the fire for warmth,
To temperate the bodies for the days,

With the days cut short,
Nights consuming more of time,
The soft beams of morning spreading,
Soaking the carpet with the morning beams,
For little warmth to drive away the chills,
The chills of winter mornings,
Slowly leaving the atmosphere,
To warm up for day's work,
The farmers leaving for the fields,
To reap the produce,
Good times for the earth,
It is the cooling time of mother earth,
The switches of nature's,
Air conditioners put on,
The whole commune in the free zone,
Cooling the heart, body, mind & soul for peace to hone,

....

(58)

The Seasons of India...

....

The Six seasons,
Twelve months,
Each season has two months,
Mother earth on one side,
The six seasons on one side,
When the earth takes a round,
The seasons smile with their faces around,
First comes the summer,
The two months sun does not spare,
The acute heat of summer burns,
Burns every one of the earth.
The insects to centipedes,
Birds to animals,
Animals to men,
Everybody runs for shadows,
For shades & cooling shelters.
Follow rains,
The incessant rains downpour,
Flood the rivers,
Wet the mother earth,
The crops, flora & fauna,
Get the nature's bath,
From clouds covering the blue skies,
To lightening showing & shining sparkles,
To thunders roaring & clouds clashing,

Umbrellas on each head,
When rain leaves,
Follows the autumn,
The beautiful autumn bring clear skies,
Patches of white clouds adorning the blue skies,
Autumn flowers blooming,
Leave spreading their wings,
Neither hot nor cold,
The pre-winter season,
With winter preludes showing up,
More of autumnal characters,
Lot of dry leaves flood the pathways
Lingering for earth's rejuvenation.
Winter comes after autumn,
The colder breeze start flowing,
The snows start falling,
The dews start dropping,
The ice clad mountains show their majestic faces,
With clouds vanishing from the skies,
Life takes a break under the covers,
Every one runs for a wrapper,
For a blanket for escaping from jaws of cold.
The pre-winter season,
That is called the Hemant Ritu (autumn),
It shows its face from November,
To the middle of December.
Spring follows the winter,
The cuckoo arrives,

Fills the atmosphere with its melody,
Coo it sings,
Such soothing to the ears,
The mango trees start flowering,
The cuckoo filters its voice chords,
Swift breeze with fragrant flowers,
Move in the atmosphere
Every wears a romantic blazer,
The five seasons as per English calendar,
During their two months sojourns each,
Bath the mother earth to its tunes,
Each giving a change to the nature,
Nature sings the chords of the particular season,
With the seasonal attributes echoing,
A tribute in the form of festivals,
Comes with each season,
With each season reigning it's rule on planet earth.

....

(59)

The Void ...

The void is beyond
Comprehension,
Beyond any understanding,
The void creates,
A wide gap,
Difficult to bridge.
Creates a distance,
Distance that gasps,
For bridging,
The small holes,
It punches,
Digging the coffin,
For the feelings,
To be dumped,
Laid to rest,
Forever,
When the void starts bridging,
The gaps start ceasing,
Everything gone.
Gone with the wind.
Leaving no trace,
No sign,
Giving shock for a life time.

(60)

The Beeline...

A beeline
That home bound Birds make,
The canvass of the blue skies.
The horizon.
The sun in the western sky
Setting for the dusk.
Before the evening falls.
A void between the day & the evening is created.
A picturesque tree looking sky bound,
An awesome sojourn takes place.
In the soul,
Oblivion to transcend,
To descend to the point of serenity.

(61)

The Waiting ...

....

The Waiting never ends..
I slept the night,
With doors open ajar,
But none came,
Neither you,
Whom I waited the night long,
The thief of my heart,
You do not come to steal my jewels,
Kept bare open,
The languish,
The anguish,
The sufferer knows better,
You are the reason,
You are the cause,
Without a cause.
Nothing works here,
Waiting ends in waiting,
To a sleepless night,
Hopes still stand aloft.
One day,
One night,
will be there.
Lest how many,
Nights I wait in between.

....

(62)

Memoir for the Nanny...

Salutes to Nanny,
That was childhood.
Under the custody of nanny,
The commands of nanny,
Obey the Ten Commandments,
Else the nanny leaves you hungry,
Locks the house,
Pressing the soft cheeks,
Thrash the soft dimple.
Books always lie idle,
When asked,
Requests rejected.
Complaints went to deaf ears.
Making me dumb.
Work hard said nanny.
Clean the backyard.
Cut the crops.
Go to fields.
Lift the soil buckets.
Fill the holes in the backyard.
Fill the gaps of the yard.
The hard ordeals who knew.
Neither kin's,
Nor Peers who abandoned us,
At the custody of the nanny.

Still revere the nanny
Whatever she taught in harsh manners,
Taught life,
Taught to fight life,
Face life.
Abundant flows the gratitude,
To nanny for the awesome,
Job she did for us then.
Today nanny is in heaven,
Salute to you nanny for the upbringing given.

. . . .

(63)

The Banyan's Grace...

....

The Uncanny Branches of the Banyan Tree,
Invites birds,
Invites the rains,
Invites the seasons,
Invites the sea,
Invites the winds,
To rest on its,
Uncanny locks,
Uncanny barks,
One above the other,
Looks uncanny,
Long hairs of a beautiful,
Young girl standing
In mute silence,
At the sea shore for ages,
Looking at the sea.
Enjoying the swift,
Breeze of the seas.
Often people assemble,
For a capture of the view,
Of the uncanny branches,

Grown uncannily,
One above the other.
In years.
It will grow.
With its,
Hugeness.
To show,
It's mute face,
To the generations.

. . . .

(64)

The Door to Heaven..

....

The Door to Heaven.
Stands ajar,
With its welcoming flames.
On the beach.
The lifeless bodies.
Arrived there.
The tides bathing them.
With the sea water.
Flames welcoming them.
Just pass through the flame.
Burn to ashes for flying.
In vapor form to heaven.
Smokes & vapors that flew sky bound.
Carried the ashes heaven ward.
Leaving ash for the mundanely earth.
The blood relations.
Who brought the dead here.
Put fire to the dead.
To free themselves,
From attachment with the body,
when it was alive.

The last remains,
Only a palm full of ash.
To be mingled into the sacred river.
As a last wish of the dead,
Travelling to heaven,
In curled smokes.
The near relations mourning.
The loss till the eleventh day.
Ritual for forgiving,
Salvation of the soul for loss of existence,
Of the lifeless sojourn to heaven.
The First & Last journey to Heaven.

....

(65)

The Dense Surfaces.

....

The density of the youthful,
Backwaters,
Spread in huge width,
From one end to the other.
Eyes fail to capture.
The reflections.
Of the.
Huge sheet of water.
An awesome capture,
For the soul to swim,
For tranquility.
The solar rays playing,
Hide & seek,
On the surface.
with the youthful,
Ripples of the sea.
Glistening in full bloom.
Fully blown like a beautiful,
Virgin lying wet.
Transparent on the huge,
Canvas of the fathomless,
Depth & Density of the waters.

....

(66)

Infant Dreams...

. . . .

Fiddling with thumb,
The child sucks,
Time passes by,
Deleting the moments,
From the chapters of life,
Life was playing.
Hide & Seek.
In the backyard of time.
The backyard was empty.
Life was cold.
With no support to hold.
The act was repeating.
Time & again.
Rejoice.
They were shouting.
But they were nowhere there.
Neither,
Time.
Nor the fiddling child.

. . . .

(67)

The Eternal Ambiguity.

....

The Eternal Question,
First came the matter,
Then came the ether.
Followed by substance.
A mystery.
Till date in puzzles.
When mind puzzles,
The eggs first or the chicken.
The seeds first or the plant.
Who arrived first?
To multiply in the planet.
So fast at such pace.
Wherever you throw a look?
Packed space of life.
Flora, Fauna and the Species,
The question remains.
Shrouded in mystery.
Who First...?

....

(68)

Drawing the Lines..

. . . .

The Artistic Journey.
The lines drawn.
A boatman with the oars.
A village belle perched on the boat.
Sailing in the river of time.
To Destinations unknown.
With the absurd pictures,
Drawn on the background.
The blue skies.
The Radiant Sun in saffron.
Glowing on the blue apron.
The handles of the oars.
Not reaching the depth.
Of the river beneath.
The fathomless touch,
Beyond the oar's reach.
The destinations.
The Fathomless depths.
Balancing the faith,
The solitary woman
in trance state.

Reaping the beauty of the sails.
Sailing & piercing into the vacuum,
Of the river beneath.
Space above,
The green grass,
With the pastures.
Wearing the sketches,
Of the artist's mind.

....

(69)

The Blank Verse

....

The Poetic Woes.
The blank mind.
Barren moods.
The Barren mind,
Becomes a devil's
workshop.
The mind needs occupation.
Blankness leads to nowhere.
The mind gets idle.
Regret.
At the predicament.
Thoughts abort.
Fail to conceive.
But sometimes,
Thoughts take time to conceive.
The mind behaves like a barren field.
Depressant thoughts.
Capturing the moods.
The poet's hope.
Mourning,
In the bay of penance.

....

(70)

Memories..

Love, Pain and Memories.
The heart has no treasuries.
Except the memories.
Pain only.
Remember the night before,
We left each other.
There was a tempest.
Blew till next dawn,
Wall erected between each other.
Separated for ever.
Suffer the pangs lifelong.
The heart bleeds even today.
Invisible.
Showing it's traces since then.
Following desertion.
From the point,
Just walk back.
The traces of the affair.
Still exist.
Never thought desertion.
But words of hurt,
Blew the tempest.
In minutes destroyed.

Today.
A face of white beards,
Dry looks of a lost philosopher.
Succumbing depth of silence.
From then,
Your rude manners,
wrought wounds after wounds.
At existence.
Surviving the onslaughts.
To ruin me,
To destroy me,
For the one,
Simple mistake of mine.
A capital punishment.
The Banishment.
But never mind,
To suffer the wounds,
To die a happy death.
Paying the penance of life.
To make you feel happy.
Breathe Happy.

. . . .

(71)

Being & Nothingness..

....

The Being.
The Nothingness.
When The being's pride,
Boasts the self.
The Nothing.
Just,
Non-existent,
The Nihilistic Philosophy.
Approach of life.
Life,
Nothing.
A Zero,
The Big Zero.
Baffles existence.
The Universe.
At crossroads.
Feigning it's falsehood,
Existence a big puzzle,
Amidst Big Wonders,
Hiding within the vast Universe,
To sustain,
The onslaught.
Within Existence.
Every moment.

An invasion,
Taking place,
Still the Universe,
Exists,
With its tortures,
Pain & Happiness,
Accepting the huge burden.
With Heart absorbing,
Accepting the tolerance,
Coining the word.
The Being and the Nothingness,

. . . .

(72)

The Dawn Arrives..

Arrive before the dawn wakes up,
Come home
Oh!
Non-entity,
Non-existent.
Come home.
For my waiting,
Not go vain.
With your arrival.
The budding petals,
In my garden bloom.
Arrive before the Sun wakes up.
Before the dawn.
A Telepathic sickness.
At Dawn.
Arrive fast.
Arrive soon.
Before it's dawn...
Before.
The Birds wakeup call

(73)

Editing

. . . .

The Editors obsession with words,
Edit the words,
The commas,
The full stops,
The grammars,
The semi colons,
The colons,
Life has lot of grammar,
Lots of colons,
The present tense,
The past imperfect,
Future perfect,
Present continuous,
If one comma,
One full stop,
One semi-colon,
wrongly placed.
The Grammar feels bruised,
Correct,
The meanings.
Taking an absurd turn.
At times easy,
At times spelling,
Real doom with,
Present past and the future.

The Editor's one simple mistake.
Turns blasphemous.
A cell of darkness.
A dungeon.
The editor locks himself,
Looks at the self.
What went wrong?
Repenting the acts,
In Silence,

....

(74)

Drunken Moods

. . . .

Drink the feelings,
From the loaded can,
In embrace,
Within closed eyes,
Moments harvested.
Frenzied feelings,
Frenzied moods,
Soul in captivity,
The beloved's wonderful vest,
The Heartbeats playing the beats.
The Lady Chatterley's lover,
Cracking the lover,
Breaking the beloved,
Gasping for breaths,
In airtight cocoons,
The breathe not halting,
Entwining serpents,
Sounds resemble the horse steps,
The Needle pins,
Pricking the points,
Breaking the joints,
Giving a sensuous hungry appetite,
The hunger never quenches,
Building trenches,
Drink the nectar,
As much as you can,
A momentous Union,

A Moment's bliss,
In solitude,
In Unison,
Breathing peace,
Breathing solace,
All tickling, curdling & boiling.
Since the dawn.
Civilization.
Tickling, boiling &curdling,
The trail of the lover's.
Burning the Cupid act of flames.

....

(75)

The Goddess of Wealth...

Invoke the goddess.
In December's beats.
Alight Oh! Goddess.
The women folk.
Of the village.
Amid the chills of the winter,
From early in the dawn,
Plastering the gaps.
With cow dung,
Soil & water mix.
Purified sacred Dreams.
Decorate the entrance of the home.
With pictures from the rice paste.
The sacred feet of the Goddess.
At the entry point.
Invoking Goddess,
Thursdays.
December's celebrity on Thursdays.
Painting the front entrances,
Mesmerizing invite for the Goddess.
House-full of wealth.
Peace and prosperity.
In True Faith.

A Festival invoking the Goddess of Wealth "Mahalaxmi"
is celebrated throughout the state on all Thursdays
falling in the month of December (Margasira). The
women folk gets totally involved in the celebration
with sweet cakes prepared from the rice to wheat
with coconut powder mince with sugar mix.

(76)

The Lap of Time...

....

Memories.....in the lap.
Bridging the gap.
Between you & me.
Boil lukewarm.
The vapors of love.
Formed droplets.
Evaporating skyward,
Mingling into the clouds.
Love in vapor.
Beyond the thick layer's.
Hiding in cloud envelopes.
Come back with the rain drops.
To the earth,
Soak the breathes.
Kiss the plants,
Swim with the rivers,
Into the seas,
Swimming with the beloved.
With the currents,
Brush with tidal currents.
Tying the couplets into words.
Memories of the sailing tides.

Mingle to the vastness.
Into dreams of transparency.
Washing the dirty linen,
Dusty lanes,
Dusty layers,
In the clean waters,
In the lap of beloved.

....

(77)

Hiccups ...

My poems.
Instill life,
Instill confidence into me.
If I do not write a day,
I can't have my sleep.
Words come in my dreams,
In dreams I write them,
I compose them,
Listen them.
Compliments flow in,
for the wonderful write,
But when I wake up,
I forget the words,
The lines composed.
Curse the sleep,
Why could not I write them?
Missing the incredible lines.
A wonderful tribute for me...
Alas!

(78)

The Whispering Silence..

....

The whispering silence,
of the moods,
of the atmosphere,
With solitude reigning,
The soul fits into the ambience.
Sinks into the solitude.
Fathomless depths.
To the dense whispers.
Where none but you,
You and me looking at the amber,
Looking at the rainbows of the horizon,
Touch of whispers,
Shadow images,
Walking the ramp,
With moon beams flashing,
on the emerald island.
The emerald island,
Whispering minds,
Bathing with the moon beams,

Beautiful beaming whispers,
With body and soul,
Kissing the beautiful moods,
The moods bathing in the soul's lagoon.
The echoes of the whispers
Heard on the turfs of the silence.

. . . .

(79)

The Ornithologist...

....

An avid bird watcher,
Passionate follower of the birds,
The life of birds.
Imitating the voices.
The birds came.
He loved them.
Far & near from the forests,
Sojourn continued,
From lakes to rivers,
From rivers to the dense forests,
Moved to listen.
Voices that sheltered in him.
In his soul,
Not a hunter,
A great lover of the birds,
Flew like them from place to place,
Leaving traces of the wings,
On the pastures of the quest,
Pastures of his hunger,
for the beautiful birds,
Who never spoke their woes?

....

(80)

Cheated by the World..

. . . .

The innocent,
A victim of cheat,
Cheated of dreams,
Cheated of present,
Cheated of past,
Cheated of future dreamt of.
Cheated by passions,
Do not forget the line ever,
Much of our pain is self-chosen.
Purely a choice of your own
Why blame others,
The thieves who snatch,
Hard earned dreams,
The pickpockets who prick holes in dream,
The roots have their nexus,
since ancient times,
The gap between man & man,
One different from another,
While one rides a Rolls Royce,
The other rolls with no choice.
Not a morsel of grain for him in universe.
Move near a temple,
Near a mosque,
Near a church,

For a morsel with verse,
The morsel the other of its species drop to him,
God does not feed,
Helpless creatures in god's domain.
Where has he to go?
A victim of circumstances,
A thief by profession.
Just think for a moment
How you stole life?
Uncertainty thy name.
From birth till death you keep chasing life.
Life becomes a victim of your targets.
Your innocence the culprit.
No regrets then,
No repentance then.
This life it means like this,
Accept them as they come.
For you are not going to carry anything,
Your materialism with you.
Just while stealing the moments,
How can you blame another.
When we all remain busy,
Stealing the moments of our choice.

....

(81)

The Divine Nectar ...

....

The nectar from the mother,
Flows abundant for the child to suck,
A divine link between the mother and the child,
Bridges the placental bond of life,
The ignorance is bliss,
Comes exhibiting,
The mom feels the ecstasy,
feeding her own,
Mother's milk for the child,
Nature's nectars,
The mother does not know the source,
But like a stream from the little mountain,
It flows relentless till the child gains wisdom teeth,
The child chews, sucks & gets drunk,
To sleep in the lap of divinity,
The mother's eternal link,
The ambrosia of milk,
Continues with infinite love,
Rearing the child to adulthood,
The child is the father of man.
A tribute to mother,

The child always beseeches the mother,
Even when grown up,
Even in all adulthood,
Mother is the emblem consecrated
in the soul of the child,
The mother & child an eternal bridge of nature,
Man a silent witness.
To the invisible threads of nature.

....

(82)

The Tired Eyes..

. . . .

With tired eyes,
Packed with sleep,
Needs a lap to exhaust,
Express the dreams,
In the fathomless,
Bed of slumber,
Sleeping into the deep,
Deep bed of gravity,
Till the tired eyes
Exhaust the sleep,
Before slipping into,
The normal routine,
Menu driven world,
Wake up,
Finish one by one
The rituals,
Brushing,
Gargling,
Cleaning the eyes,
Face for the day to start...

. . . .

(83)

The Conflicting Mind...

....

The conflicts of the mind...
Does not leave me,
Does not allow me
to leave my passions,
Caught between the
two ends
my revolting soul,
cries for solace,
Whether to remain with passions
pursue or not,
Living with passion is such easy,
Living without it just nigh possible,
Just few days few nights
Leaving without my passion,
My love for my creativity
A wrong choice for my soul
Kept me throttling with questions,
How can you?
A just abnegation no solution
Rude to love,
Passions your poems,
Just Write them.

Write the genuine feelings.
From the cocoon's self,
Tears in the eyes.
Convert them to pearls my dear,
They say me,
Yes my love,
I am your lover,
I am the passion,
I am life,
Never leave soon,
Live with you,
Die without you,

....

(84)

The Warring Mind..

....

The warring mind,
Always fights,
Fighting with the stomach.
Fighting with existence.
Fighting with conscience.
A picture keeps occupying.
When one want is satisfied,
Other crops up in its place,
Well known truth,
Hidden in law.
One chocolate,
Giving real satisfaction,
Eating more diminishes.
The Appetite.
With the satisfaction graph.
No more.
No more.
One want when satisfies.
Another follows suit,
Too much bores.
It is nature.
The eternal questions.
Asked since time immemorial.

As we search,
The truth time & again.
Ends in conclusion,
The endless cold wars,
Fought by war mongers,

. . . .

(85)

The Summing up..

....

Some poems are wonderful.
From start to summing up,
They contain the amazing themes,
Imaginations of the poetic mind.
Infuses life into them.
The poet infuses life to the words.
Bewildering the Reader.
The missiles in the messages.
Touches everyone.
From the lover to the mercenary.
Transmitting the words to symbols.
Handcuffing memories.
Creating milestones.
The reader reaps the words,
Harvesting words into golden letters...
Weighing the depth.
Only some write them,
Read them,
Understand them.

To understand the meaning of life.
The meaning of love,
Convert the words,
To immortal feelings,
Carve a niche in the soul,
In pursuit of the real.

. . . .

(86)

The Point of No Return..

Every wave that touches the shore,
Recedes back into the depth of the ocean.
The fathomless bed ashore,
Every bird that flies away,
Returns homeward before the evening falls.
To the Starting point.
From where it flew to count.
Touch after the round.
The perimeter of existence.
The eyes of the universe,
Even fixed, shines.
The sun lighting the universe with radiant beams.
The moon lighting the universe with cool beams.
Start every day.
Return every evening.
To the same point.
The law that rules the universe.
In all paradox life.
A Black & White game in rife.
Shadows hiding in the verse,
In the Universe.
Where each word has an opposite.
Each action.
Has an equal & opposite reaction.
The nine planets in rotation.
Balance the earth from outside,
Hanging in space.

An invisible rope of gravity.
That holds the earth along its axis.
The inhabitants take a telescopic view,
of the planetary rotation.
Each word has an opposite.
Birth has death as it's opposite.
The male has female as his opposite.
The opposite attraction,
An eternal truth.
A magnetic force binds the opposites into existence.
The hidden truth everything that goes comes back.
But when life goes it comes back as death.
The life that breathes but the dead is stale...
The opposite of real is unreal.
What a paradox.
What an universal truth.
Go & come to the same point.

....

(87)

Golden Harvest

Just look at the golden radiance,
The clouds turning into gold,
The horizon bathing golden,
The awesome fire line reflections,
On the water beneath,
The golden spectacles,
The green trees bowing their leaves,
Honoring the serene ambience,
Transcendence walking ramp,
On the surrounding,
Lifting the veils of the Nature,
The horizon throwing a hillock,
To resist the tempestuous,
The golden fusion spraying its shadows,
Making the scenic alight on earth,
The sublime divine quenching
The unrequited passions,
Intense enlightenment in reality.

(88)

The Master Strokes,

. . . .

When you whistled your voice,
Into the tiny holes of your flute,
The village girl dances.
To the mellifluous tunes,
In the magic voice of the flute,
Rested existence,
The meaning of life,
When your magic tunes kissed their ears,
Their heart & soul danced to the tunes,
Forgetting the worldly attachments,
Merging into your sublime plays,
To fiddle with you,
Oh! Lord of the Flute.

. . . .

(89)

Blind Love

....

Blind love,
A mad passion,
Fanatic madness,
Uncompromising attitudes,
The love exists,
None else,
Excepting the blind attachment.
The blind threads tying,
Invisibly,
Building the cobweb,
The cocoon,
The bird's nest,
The anthills,
A home for stay,
But love for passion,
The threads invisible,
Binds love,
Invisible threads,
At times
Wonder at the situation,

Whether I deserve so much,
So much love,
That pores in,
It is nothing,
But Blind love.

. . . .

(90)

The Child Prodigy...

....

A Child prodigy,
A True Genius,
The paper boats of childhood,
Still make their sail,
In memory,
In the rainy waters,
They sailed,
My paper boats,
In folds of the boat,
Lived my art & crafts,
I waited for rains
The whole year to arrive.
When rains arrived,
With the first showers,
My joys just unleash limitless,
My mind just tress-passes.
To the corridors in silence,
Dwells in rains
Sans umbrella,
Dances to the drizzling drops,
Till it soaks the soul.

I run for a piece of paper,
A piece of torn paper,
From my note book,
Created a paper boat,
Sailed it in the waters,
Running to the sewerage.
Dance in ecstasy
At the creative supermanship.
The child dancing like an adult.
For a moment.
A creative genius,
Till the paper boat sailed to a watery grave.

. . . .

(91)

Repentance....

....

Repenting on the bank of time,
On the bark of the tree,
Engrave the symbolic heart,
With the sharp nails of the knife,
The bark was bleeding with pain,
But no care,
When memories of you hunt me,
I run there,
Visit the tree look at the bark,
The tree has forgotten the small wound,
I carved on it,
The engraving has grown in size,
Looks magnified with its symbolic prize,
The engraving only reminds my madness,
That existed during youth,
When nothing but love,
Reigned in truth,
Silently bowing to the bark,
If Love is a crime We committed it.
In life,
Atoning today,
Repenting silently on the bank of time,

....

(92)

Galaxy...

....

The starry nights.
Throw a look at the galaxy tonight,
The stars twinkling at the earth,
Earth presenting itself at the starry nights,
The starry nights flashing smiling stars.
Amidst planets flashing million watts,
The soul traversing through the galaxy's huge carpet,
The huge carpet of starry nights.
Dim-lit darkness with a glass of wine catching the moods,
The thinker, the writer, the poet & the lover bathing,
One mind but varied presentations,
In the lagoon of the starry nights,
All stars wearing a mermaid's look,
With the planets smiling,
With the moon throwing it's tantrums,
The cool beams to love beams.
For the lovers to soothe,
Melting into each other.
A lily smiling in the rippling pond,
Soul swimming with the ripples,
The nature much appealing,
To take a dip in the space's emptiness,
Lull for a moment winking at the stars,
Solitude of the open sky in score,

....

(93)

The Cobweb of Life,

....

The Cobweb of life,
Like a cobweb,
Two hundred six bones,
Presenting a cobweb.
The skeleton,
With a head atop,
With grey matter,
With two eyes for vision,
A nose to breathe,
Two hearing aids.
A heart inside beating like the clock.
Beating the drum of life,
round the clock.
At times for the beloved,
It's special beats
music for life.
Life into the body put by the stomach,
The intestines the toilet for the body to reject excreta.
The pelvic guards mining the seeds.
Frozen seeds,
Future to breed.

....

(94)

Ablutions...

When you wash the dirt,
Purify the body,
Take a dip in the holy waters,
With sacred chants,
Purify the mind,
Sanctity of the body.
What an act of travesty,
When one washes the body for purity,
How does one wash the soul?
Is it the sacred chants,
For the Soul to purify?
Chanting sacred lines,
Ablute the soul.

(95)

The Dark Traces..

....

The pulse halts for a moment,
But time moves non-stop.
The Pilgrimage on.
Soul seeks umbrage.
Walking step after step,
Started long-long ago.
Pilgrim of the planet,
A Monk in the monastery,
Lamps burning.
Pouring oil into the lamp of life,
The wick flickering with every breathe,
The fire burns passionately the oil of life.
The thread of life.
The wick burning happily,
The thread born to burn,
The wick's life breathes fire,
The oil the symbolism in source.

....

(96)

The Moratorium,

. . . .

The gap in time,
When thoughts simply do not alight,
Forget to alight from the galaxy,
The mind dives sky ward,
When the poet's supersonic speed,
Flies sky bound towards the galaxy,
To swim amidst the twinkling stars,
The moon & planets.
Once in space the vacuum such absorbing.
The mind does not alight from galaxy,
From the nebula,
Amidst the huge pasture of the galaxy,
The Soul lightening like a mirage in a desert,
Searching the Oasis,
The Mirage,
Life in galaxy,
The moratorium clears.
Clouds dispersing
The blue sky opening it's blues,
That spread abound,
Imagine beyond & beyond.
The canvass of the mind.
In true delight.

. . . .

(97)

Mystery of Evolution,

....

The Evolution of Man,
Masterpiece in creation,
A shadow of the MASS universe,
The Bridge lying in between,
Between the MINI & the MASS,
Replication in multitudes.
Every man differs from the other,
Everyone a genius par excellence,
The genesis not known so far,
Mysteries of the universe,
Hidden inside,
It's dual appearance a stark reality,
Visible but often forgotten,
The black & white faces,
Shrouded mysteries,
Since time immemorial,
Human search the depths,
The evolution.
The Events.

A shrouded affair treasured inside the universe.
None to explain the affair.
From great saints to philosophers.
Each explaining in their own way.
Secrets that remain shrouded.
Vanish into the realm of infinity.
The surreal universe the mysterious existentialism.
All shrouded in the folder of time.

. . . .

(98)

An Evening with You...

Fluid moments...
The evenings with you,
Such amazing,
Spend time,
Forget the world,
In the moonlit night,
When moon baths us,
Penetrating the beams
Into the silken glows,
The silken pearls,
Glowing with beauty,
The beams in romance,
Making moods flash,
With smile sending,
A shiver down the spine,
With shrill voice your moans,
Echoing,
The surrounding,
For moments the closed eyes,
Never knew when we became one,

A Balloon in heart,
Life moving in togetherness.
Caressing the lover.
Mind's fluid state.
Something inside,
Something outside,
Soul kissing the mind.

....

(99)

BLISSHOOD...

....

As the night grows deeper,
Darkness of the density grows thicker,
The creepers to humans,
Everyone goes into the world of slumber,
The world of slumber,
The woes of man becomes lesser,
Slumber takes away man's worries,
Tiresomeness of the day's hard labour,
Man slips into the world of unconscious,
Into the dreamland where slumber
takes away the conscious,
In the lap of slumber love to hide,
The beautiful landscapes that take
him inviting for a joyful ride.
The lagoons & the mermaids choosing his stride.
Like a log of dead wood the body sleeps.
Totally in a world of unconsciousness.
Life does not desert him even from his eternal bliss.
In his utter helpless body lies like a log of wood.
Night takes life into the nocturnal esoteric zones,
The body lies like a log of wood snoring the dreams.
The soul romancing with slumber.

....

(100)

TRUE BLISS, TRUE JOY.

....

Joy,
Enjoy.
Enjoy the bliss,
Bliss is surreal,
Surreal is sublime,
Sublime is oblivion,
Oblivion is transcendence,
Transcendence is meditation,
Meditation is monkhood,
Monkhood to Godhood.
Joy is the magnetic healer.
That heals human sorrows,
Human wounds,
Giving the healing touches,
Enjoy the blissful space,
Embalm the soul with solace,
With peace,
Surreal a true surrender,
In sublime hood hides,
The enigma of life,
Oblivion the unique transfused peace,
The soul to realize the hidden truths,
Transcendence the journey in meditation,
Meditation & monkhood complimenting each other,
The link between the matter & non-matter,
The universe a battle zone of confusion.

Confusing minds & thoughts,
Between war & peace,
Violence & non-violence,
Truth & lie,
Black & white,
Light & darkness,
Dwells the meanings,
Neither war is a winner,
Nor violence,
Nor lie or darkness,
It is attitudes of confused minds,
Confused thoughts,
Peace alone,
Non-violence alone,
Truth alone,
Light alone can bring joy,
Bring true happiness,
Bring true peace,
Bring true BLISS.

....

(101)

The Depth of Feelings..

....

Silent Feelings,
Clasping palms,
Crossed fingers,
In deep embrace,
Closed eyes,
Cooked up feelings,
Romance in swing,
Hisses of the soul,
Blowing past the mind,
The mind in regale moods,
The beloved's clasp,
Takes away the breathes,
The lover feels sandwiched,
Between the pace of sighs,
Furnace fire & the molten lava,
Of the embracing frames,
Throttled existence,
The magic moments,
Cascading moods,
Layers over layers,
Over the soul's blind grounds,
The breathes & groans,
Music to the drums,

Beating with fast rhythmic cycles,
Losing the depth,
Sinking beyond the fathomless,
The soul swimming in joy,
Engrossed silence,
Engrossed happiness,
An obsession for the lover's
Since time immemorial,
Hold on.
Hold on for a moment.
The clasp will burst the heat.
Bring peace to the lover's.

....

(102)

As You unfold...

. . . .

When you reveal.
Yourself.
You really heal.
The accumulated woes.
Undress the soul's robes,
Disrobe the mind.
To allow it find,
The nude truths,
Hidden inside the mouth,
When the grey matter opens up.
The true revelations comes up.
You wait for story to publish.
Without caring the fuss,
For that sake give your soul a kiss.
Revealing is a daring act for self to embrace peace.
No one dares to reveal the dark effects,
Because everyone enjoys remaining perfect,
This world surrounded with false images,
Lies one above the other told without brakes,
The teller does not know the no. of lies told,
The counter keeps an account of the lies told,
The more you tell lies,
The more you succeed,
For that matter the liar never pays any heed.

. . . .

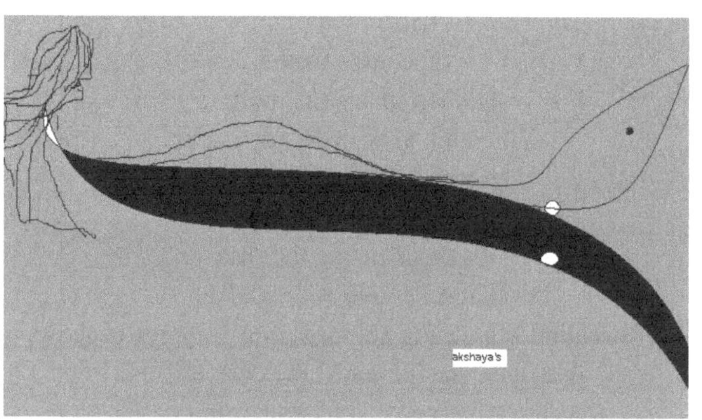
akshaya's

(103)

Curves of the Nymph...

. . . .

The curved beauty.
Nymph of time,
The beautiful beaks with curves.
The pointed long beaks.
The powerful lenses.
The curved beak.
With the beautiful bird's fins.
The lake beneath.
Feet firmly perched.
The blueness of the canopy.
Is the only answer to the horizon?
The mysterious world full of curves,
Curves are always dangerous.
Dangerous for the moving life.
Dangerous to the eyes,
Wild feelings roaring like lions,
Man losses self-esteem,
Negotiates the curves,
The curvy roads,
The curvy cunning circles,
Runs towards the caves secrecy,
For privacy,
Curves eternally play a role,

Acting secretly for the man's love for the mole,
From the curvy bird to man,
Every one runs towards the curves,
For the mind & eyes to quench,
The thirst for beauty,

....

(104)

The Rebels.

....

All those pains,
Wrought on the face of society,
All those evils,
Wrought on the face of the humanity,
The voice of rebel,
The voids that society created,
Never taking the name of ending,
A revolution brews inside,
The rebellion preparing for the onslaught,
Capitalism spreading its roots deep,
The name of communism gone to sleep,
From the dictionary of humanity,
Lot of hunger,
Disease,
Abuse of man by man,
Children malnourished,
Life getting tougher for the poor,
The rich relishing lavish,
The Gap of divide.
The difference between man & man,
Between nations widening every minute.

Peace procrastinated for all time,
In the name of peace man busy bullying,
Bullying own brethren & species,
What a sad state of affair,
When one cries for little alms,
The other destroys granaries of surplus,
No concern & conscience exists,
The rebellion offers no answer,
The calamity gives birth to rebel,

....

(105)

The Tweets of the Incomprehensible..

....

The incomprehensible,
Voice they tweet.
The bird's language.
Solicit the partner for talk,
A talk about the small family.
To negotiate the moments.
Pecking & sneaking into each other.
Every minute they tweet.
Tweet in the voice.
The voice soliciting birds.
To assemble on the dense branches.
The huge banyan tree packed with leaves.
Overcrowded in moments.
No one knows.
Where from they come,
Where they go?
They just assemble to tweet,
Sing their songs sweet,
Putting love mates into hypnosis,
Hypnotizing frenzied moods,
No one knows,
In the little domain,
Eggs,
Drop, warm & incubate.

Little off springs just start to tweet.
Both move & collect.
Food stuff for the little kids born to them.
The bird's community rejoicing.
In community felicity.
Felicitating the new born to the domain,
To the world of life,

…………………………………………

(106)

The Black Pagodas (Konark)

The Stone-art of Konark.
Mesmerizing images of masonry,
Silent testimony of time,
When sharp nails,
Cut into beautiful,
Images of lovers.
Enlivening young erotica,
Imagining adolescence,
Embracing the beloved's,
Thoughts of love,
On the engrave,
On the solid rock pieces,
From images of god,
To Goddesses,
Nude polished granite images,
The sharp nails of the augurs,
Breathing life into the figures,
Touching the soul of the rocks,
The hard rocks coated with lust,
Depicting art,
Love, Lust & Sex in them,
A silent monument,

Mute for ages,
Since the twelfth century,
The huge granite edifice,
One wonders,
In silence,
Visitors struck with the masonry,
The classics of love,
Nudity of stone images,

....

"Konark" Temple in Odisha, India is one wonderful stone architect of ancient architecture in stone carving. Building the temple in 12 th Century facing the Bay of Bengal 1200 Masons were engaged by the King to complete the gigantic stone work.

The depictions in stone carvings show picture of love making in varied forms with huge stone wheels surrounding the temple like a chariot. Legend says that Dharmapada son of one of the mason who fixed the temple's top & jumped into the ocean to save the head of 1200 masons who would have faced Death for not able to complete the Temple top within time.

(107)

The Hibernation..

....

She goes hiding into hibernation,
The request still pending to be written.
She leaves me in annoyance,
Could not write a poem in flamboyance.
The topic such a riddle,
Think, think & fiddle.
The thoughts so hard,
Moods always went dried.
Not easy to think,
Lest the poem would have come with eye's blink.
A poem on blood cancer in conception.
The mind does not obey the thoughts situation.
Blood cancer requires periodic blood transfusion.
The platelets count downward syndrome.
Donor's crisis makes it the patient to roam.
The other option bone marrow transplantation.
The cost & the facility need a thorough discussion.
Life becomes a real challenge for the patient.
The patient needs to be more patient.
Hold patience & persevere to face.
The ordeal of periodic blood transfusions to brace.
The heart needs to be brave.
The calamity needs to a save.

Sympathy with compassions.
Life becomes a puppets play of daily confessions.
At times eyes become red.
Needs super specialty medication in bed.
It is better to surrender, succumb to the disease.
Than making an attempt to end the crisis.
It is the dreaded blood cancer.
Which needs patience & periodic
blood & platelets transfer?
Live life as it goes,
Worries do not land you any solution near,
Better surrender to the Omni-powerful God for a better,
Transcription.
Only in him lies the solution.
If thee wants.
Thee can draft the total cure without medication.

....

(A Poem on Blood Cancer on request by a follower.)

(108)

In Memoriam..

....

Still those blood red eyes.
Jostle before eyes,
So young.
A friend who died young.
After a decade write a memoriam.
In just seven days left the aquarium.
The aquarium of life sailed.
Just half way lifted him body & soul as failed.
Cancer in blood never could be imagined.
In seven day' s time everything was over.
Leaving the family & recuperating old dad from fever.
Mother was speechless,
Wife not in senses,
Little son could not understand the mess,
At times God too becomes cruel,
The burial ground readying for the fuel,
At such young age death snatches away,
Friends & relatives really aghast,
No option than lay the body to rest,
In moments the body in flames,
In minute's body in ash,

Watching as mute & silent spectator,
Help nowhere in sight,
Excepting the family mourning the plight,
In love with Death,
Death in love with his hearth,
Nearly a decade gone,
Somewhere down the memory the events burn,

....

(A poem written in memory of a friend
who died of blood cancer.)

(109)

The Chirping Birds.

....

Hopping,
Jumping,
Flying,
Sitting,
From branch to branch,
In between,
The tweets,
The pecking,
The seeking,
Entwining,
Seeds injected,
No one knows,
When the eggs,
Dropped,
Formed,
Building a nest for the little children,
The male bird,
Collects the dry pieces of straw,
To weave the grove,
To nurture the eggs,
Incubate them,
Hope is born.

....

(110)

Daughters...

....

They are my daughters,
My life, my pulse & stars in clusters,
Love their dad immortal,
Doting daughters forgiving dad's acts of mortal.
Dad, Dad, Dad they come running.
One on the neck.
One on the shoulders.
The other on the back keep turning.
The love they pour.
From the soul's stock.
Keeps the Dad's battery running,
Life becomes truly meaningful.
Heavenly foundations of learning,
The daughter's never betray the father.
Know the weakness & strength of the father.
Take care of every small need rather.
The father & the daughter.
Bound in an immortal thread.
The daughter's care more than the mother,
No difference between the daughter & the mother,
From the moment the daughter' s were born.

Luck becomes the fervor.
The father always felt gracious.
Impeccable in his attitudes towards the daughter.
The daughter always take side of the father,
A daughter a true friend.
Guide & philosopher to the father,

....

(111)

Drunken Amber...

. . . .

Drunken lips.
Drunken kisses.
On beautiful faces.
Leaves traces.
Saliva traces.
Love is wild.
Never get wild.
The heart filled.
The mind gets reeled.
The soul gets chilled.
The lover's gaze.
Gives pleasure & amazes.
Whenever in embrace.
In tight hugs hands locked.
Listen the pulse races.
Bodies trespass.
What a feel.
Moments in kill.
Killing the sighs with emotional drill.
The lovers leave a beautiful trail.
The body feels more to regale.
Life a cage.

Chapters unfold in slow page.
Lover's forever live in paradise.
Moments unfolding the treasures.
The hidden treasures,
Secret store of nature.
To be opened when mature.
The music of the soul to satires.
The will for a future.
Love is a cute torture.

....

(112)

MERRY CHRISMAS & HAPPY NEW YEAR..

....

A Merry Christmas.
When the world revels in mass prayers,
World over lot of snows.
Decorate the earth with white powders.
As if earth wears a white beard on its face.
Flora, fauna to houses & buildings carry the snow trace.
When you wake up in the morning the
mornings offers super chills.
Insects, moths, animals to humans run for blankets.
Run into shelter to hide their frail structures in the groves.
The Santa Clauses sing 25th December.
December the month of amber.
With frenzied moods of divinity & moments happier.
Every one silently bows to the other to feel merrier.
Christmas time ...time takes a nap for supper.
Souls quiver amass for Christmas Prayer.
May the world be more beautiful and merrier?
May poverty and non-violence leave the world for better?
May the guns & bombs get replaced with bread & butter?
The rich to poor unify,
Divinity just purify,
Purify the soul.
Purify the mind.

Distance between man & man diminish,
The universe can revel in joy in wind.
The chills give new frills.
Snow carpets on earth.
Man in winter costumes.
New looks,
The Christmas time.
The month long rhyme,
The sacred 25th of December,
Bind the world in one amber,
Amber of happiness, peace & Prosperity
with just seven days for NEW YEAR...
TO ALL WISHES, FELICES FIESTAS, MERRY
CHRISTMAS & HAPPY NEW YEAR

....

(113)

Man & Woman

....

God made man.
God made woman.
It is only two words that divide man from woman.
Man & woman.
Oh!
Man calls woman.
The woman calls.
Oh! Man.
We are two but ultimately ONE.
Man's love for woman,
In the woman's heart hides the real man.
The real man woman's real passion,
The hungers of the bodies.
Play like the beautiful swan.
God's wish a preordain.
Man & woman unify to create.
Procreate.
Lest the barrenness.
The children the future.
Man & woman both nurture,
Man & woman hide their treasures.
For future.
The family their creativity,
Their art and architecture.

....

(114)

At times..

....

My composition gives me a slip,
While posting the content the system suffers a trip,
Cannot remember exactly what I wrote,
Fumbling for some time to assemble the note,
The system fails to recover the content,
Curse the self for a moment,
Rethought the concept once again,
Recapitulated the lines with so much pain,
We're not the same again,
The theme could with difficulty remain,

....

(115)

Lover's & Hater's.

....

Lover's or Hater's
No matter.
I have my lover's,
Have my hater's.
Between love & hate I get treaters.
Love me abound,
Hater's hate me around,
Know my happiness & tears.
Have no fears.
I love both lover's & hater's.
No care what matters.
This is life.
Better to accept.
May what come?
No matter how come they come?
Life a big satire.
Even if one does not desire.
The long miles.
Never more than hundred miles.
Do not know who loves or who hates.

Leave them to choose.
It is purely the friend or foe's choice.
Life has always been a journey alone.
It has never any born friend or foe to hone.
Just take it easy.
Whether you feel sad or happy.
Just remain busy

....

(116)

Don't Hide me in Your Heart.

....

Do not hide in me in your heart.
Would not like to suffocate before death?
In Death I would conceal.
Ruminate with my fate's sad ordeal.
Never let one know the heart's feel.
Better burn them inside & send chill.
The ruminations would be a tribute for you.
Never let anyone down.
Life is a journey of miles.
Ups & down full of frills,
Balance life.
Love and the thrills.
No mock drills.
Mock drills put one down.
Committing the act why frown.
Good & bad all God's design.
Whatever happens.
Happens for fine.
Accept them well in time,
The world is tiny.
Miniature Space of time.
Feel baffled to sing a rhyme.
What a sordid affair to pantomime.

....

(117)

The Whispers from the soul…

……………………………………………

The soul's whispers,
Who has not heard tells lies,
The symbolic messages comes in whispers,
Whispers sounds in silent tracks,
The music of the soul play blanks,
Blank surrounding,
vacuum pranks,
In minutes over,
In matters cranks,

……………………………………………

(117)

Leave me alone...

....

Just leave me alone.
When Time is gone.
Just leave me alone.
A decade is gone.
Once we were so known.
Periodic hibernation.
Time goes for incubation.
Renew the infatuation.
The past beautiful.
Meet at the cross road' s fall.
She knew me tall.
Instantly recognized & fell.
When time was there.
You never see me for a moment.
Leave me with the surrender list,
So Broken to hold the fist.
Wonder at times why you came.
How cruel could you become?
My life is not a game of pawn.
As you wish play & run.
Run here run there.
Could find you nowhere.
Elope with a stranger.
For somewhere.

Never again saw you there.
The point of no return.
Accept the defeat like any other,
One among many& talk no more,
Same steps difficult to walk,
I am sure even if you desire.
I love not to wait here.
Make a mockery of life before the final attack.
Leave me alone,
Just leave me alone to face the attack.
The cracks of life are just irreparable better be frank.
Leave me alone to rest in peace,
Just leave the pranks,

……………………………………………

(119)

Tributes to Mother.

. . . .

Mother oh! My mother,
Where are you gone leaving us here.
The death anniversary falls this day every year,
It was 6th of January in 1994.
Calculated as per solar calendar.
Almost two decades since you left for heavenly abode.
Death snatched you to God.
Bereaved family cried & cried.
But the cruel destiny behaved fraud.
It snatched you from us to GOD.
Leaving us here to remember you every now & then.
Dad is there thirty years after even.
We pray God to rest your soul in peace.
May the soul's salvation take place?
We seek today nothing but your silent blessings.
We are yet to submerge the ash.
May Dad live more.
We will remember.
This day & pay the tributes in your honor year after year.

. . . .

(120)

The Great Book...

Life is a great book,
The face of it is a great hook,
What we see is all fake,
At times we have to put the brakes,
A sachet from where I am born,
I feel for the father.
I feel for the mother.
Father who implanted the seed.
Mother who gave me the feed.
In all smallness the tall frame,
Today stands tall in name,
Proud feelings for the father,
Hats off mother,
You gave me the upbringing,
You sang the songs I am singing.
In the huge universe.
Too small a miniature.

(121)

The Hindsight...

....

Not much change excepting age.
Life is to pass all this stage.
Only memories in the mind's page.
When the pages open one by one feel the craze.
So many people, so many places come in the stage.
Friends who knock your doors need praise.
The gaps in time need a bridge.
Old friendship & bonds renewed.
Get you moments of nostalgia to brood.
Brood over the meetings.
Brood over the sittings.
The past a good memory.
Opens up a Pandora box and a huge treasury.
Gossips never end.
When time passed could not defend,
There comes a time when you need a friend,
Confess your guilt to fend.
Before it is too late to apprehend.
Stories will remain stories in the grind.

....

(122)

Mickey Mouse...

....

Mickey & Mouse.
What a cute pose.
The tweets at wits.
The spectators get sweets.
The twins awesome.
There actions wonder for some.
When one raises a hand.
The other raises his wand,
They are twins cynosure of the grandpa & the nanny's.
The nanny just rejoice.
When the twins play gimmicks.
They are such wonders.
One thinks for a moment the other takes by surprise the bystanders.
Awesome pictures.
Amazing treasures.

....

(123)

The Reflective Mirror

....

The eye is beautiful mirror.
That reflects your picture.
The heart takes a tour.
The soul in beautiful capture.
The awesome reflects.
That touches the intellects.
The picture you have to select.

....

(124)

Likes & Dislikes...

....

Likes & dislikes are purely one's own choice.
Whether they like or dislike it's their voice.
The voice of people just matters.
Man cannot assess his own self however better.
His creations are his very choice.
Nothing can impede him from the pilgrim's progress.
Books are best friends.
Only few of them really read.

....

(125)

Temporary Universe...

. . . .

Everything in world is so temporary.
Someone survives a day.
Someone's just stay.
All that has a trace of life expire.
But the invisible just aspire.
Everything has a date.
None knows the summons of the fate.
One unique truth life is death.
When you survive life is truth.
When you die life is death.
But love is one that is faith.
Binds two souls into one trust.

. . . .

(126)

Chilling Winter

The winter gives a feel.
Without blankets just chill.
Hold the body in the tight arms.
Hide the face to feel warm.
Light little fire.
Assembly gathers sooner or later.
Warm up the body.
Before too late get ready.
Walk on the morning grass.
Shining dew drops just embarrass.
As the sun grows ageing the dew drops vanish.
Whole night they rained their wish.
Wet the mother earth cooling her dish.

(127)

The Illusions of the flash...

....

The eye and the world.
The God made lenses of wonderful mold.
Capturing the awesome pictures that rolled.
The beautiful mirror when unfold.
Stored in the library of the mind.
Amazing pictures that comes before the sight.
Amazing visions of fright.
When the mind unfolds they come so bright.
The mind's library storing pictures in the albums pit.
When posterity unfolds they take one so contrite.
In lighter moments a just look at them.
Soul bathing in the past realms.
Nostalgia flows to the brim.
Surrendering to the past charm,
Flashbacks of picture without any harm.
When Past is beyond recovery.
Past is history.

A very difficult capture.
Mind & souls stay in wonder.
Pleasant or sad with pain always surrender.
Life is yonder.
Life is a wonder.
The lenses just capture.
The false picture.
When life becomes history.
The pages of pictures become a story.

....

(128)

Wonderful Minds

. . . .

Just look at the picture.
For it is such a true wonder.
Think for a moment.
How views can torment.
Duplicate vision.
The more you look the more confusion.
The maker's choice.
The viewer just rejoice.
The manipulations.
Sheer admirations.
Think for a moment,
If life behaves so how to react?
Illusion in reality.
Photogenic reality.

. . . .

(129)

SLICE OF LOVE..

LOVE a beautiful slice.
Nothing so tasty & real spice.
The mouth waters.
Soul feels juicy.
The four lettered word.
Enters the heart forget the chords.
Life becomes hurry.
In moments life becomes a story,
Two souls lose the vision.
In embrace they go in fusion.
The fusion happens.
The chord & tabla in unison.
The players roam.
In a world of dream.
The dream a passion.
A true life mission.
Accomplished in soul's prison.

Love a beautiful season.
Lovely prison.
Time & again caught in the rain.
When caught lover's just feign.
The slice eaten.
Slave of real tan.
Possessed & obsessed.
Soul remains admitted.
Just take a slice.
Love a beautiful slice.

....

(130)

Innocent murdering...

Oh! How can it be so cruel?
Bullets for the school.
What a situation in fuel.
At last Small children.
Targeted for no fault of theirs.
Acts of terrorism.
Acts of fanaticism.
Hunts for situations.
To attack educational institutions.
What a pity.
Full of blood & ethos.
Innocent murdered.
Cold blood bath flowed.
The innocent students to teachers.
All given a blood bath to face the fury of the traitors.
The gory saga suffocate in words.
Throttle the voice to be speechless.
A tooth for the tooth.
A spade for spade they say in full mouth.
It is life how can it be battered.
In utter chaos and a child's head.

Even wild animals do not avenge.
The way a mercenaries revenge.
One hundred Forty lives shot dead.
The acts of cowardice and brutal tread.
Live cannons commanding a bow down.
Bullets at life just frown.
The dastardly act.
Needs serious evaluation.
It is difficult to eschew the event & forget the crisis.
May the innocent children stay in peace.
God forgive the wrong doers.
In such deep crisis so motto comes the prayers.
The world should unite & stand in ovation.
Cry for the soul's peace for oblation.

....

(131)

Christmas on the Anvil...

....

Christmas on the anvil.
Just happening with nature's beautiful chill.
Santa clause's on the streets on drill.
Pulling the children with their clownish looks for a thrill.
The Nature too has a new dress covering with snows full.
Leafs of the dwarf to tall trees even
green grass wears the snow
Blanket.
Mother earth warming up in its groves giving
warmth to the basket.
The basket full of amazing flowers.
Decorate the houses with beautiful towers.
Children run to shake hands with the Shanta.
No one knows what hides in the clown Shanta.
Children just madly attracted towards the Shanta Claus.
Love to remain in the fold of the Shanta's beautiful claws.
The Poor to Rich clean the selves for a befitting
Rejoice.
New colorful wears from children to adults.
Every house the Christ lives.
With Christmas Trees decorated with lights.
Cakes & pastries to sweet dishes.
Abundance flows.
As if Jesus has alighted for world to heave PEACE.

....

(132)

Life in a Tricycle...

....

Just see the happiness in the man's face,
His folded hands only say grace.
His distressed life with leprosy.
Life's strange behaviors never that rosy.
The whole life went in eking out a living.
Little alms, compassion & the profession of begging.
In his diseased state he has a family.
Disease is no definition to life for punishing the family.
His tricycle is his moving spirit of life.
He moves from door to door in strife.
Some body gives palm full of alms.
Some just do not listen to his appeals & qualms.
Life has been too harsh towards him.
The youth betrayed.
Disease taking a toll.
Never afraid of life.
Life has lessons for the world from strife.
A cursed existence that becomes.
He has to survive and live may what come...

....

(133)

Writing is a passion.....

....

For some days I am so busy.
I do not find time to sit easy.
Writing is a passion.
The very thought strikes like a reason.
I am not able to sit calm.
Just few thoughts need little qualm.
If words come in time.
I do not have to worry for the rhyme.
The preoccupations of time.
Keep me busy for no reason & rhyme.
Priorities are such preordained.
One can't avoid them, man always chained.
The reasons have an answer.
Always solve them the sooner.
Lest problems keep chasing.
Man becomes a victim all the while racing.
Life's priorities keep me bereft.
My poems could not find time to draft.
Just forgive me reader's,
Sorry for the expressions,

....

(134)

Issues in Life...

. . . .

Issues in life matters.
At times they put you in dangers.
Threat life.
One goes restless in sheer strife.
Good people often become victims.
Suffer for no fault of theirs.
When the inch-cape rock sink.
The pulse of life starts to blink.
Even you try to sail through.
It becomes tougher.

. . . .

(135)

The Test of Life...

....

Life is an acid test.
Full of surprises sweet & sour to taste.
When acid burns.
There is no flame but still one burns.
The Sad predicament one cannot afford to turn.
Events keep happening.
Truly shattering.
Dreams a man sees in life.
Turns into sour without any rife.
Repent for the mistakes.
Not enough even without any stakes.

....

(136)

Happy Events...

. . . .

Happy Events in family.
Keep happening timely.
Birthdays to marriage of children.
Time to time sure to happen.
When such events take place.
The mood of the family regale in true rejoice.
The would be' s just get confused.
Such an important event from single to double hood.
The new would be' s dream.
Her talks & manners all imagined in realm.
Sweet day dreams other than the night.
Both get lost into each-other's soul's flight.
Anxiously waiting for the event to happen.
The preludes start much in advance with lot of hyphen.
The bride & the groom wait in vain.
To accept the truths of life that happens like heaven.
The parents & relatives,
Maternal uncles, friends & aunties.

All just revel in swiveled chairs merry go rounds.
Rose, jasmine, dahlias & Orchids twinkle with their petals.
The groom to bride garlanded with all sweet murals.
Decorative foreheads with ornaments.
Adore the whole body with new garments.
The Soul goes dancing.
With music playing full blown to find everyone romancing.

....

(137)

The Christmas Flavor...

. . . .

Today half the population of the world goes rejoicing.
The Christmas Eve is celebrated
around the world in full swing.
The Churches are beautiful decorated.
The religious rituals in honor of the Lord.
The world is in beautiful mood.
The western hemisphere celebrates the big day.
The day starts growing bigger from today.
In chilled winters the world goes reeling.
Tom & Jerry to Pantaloons give a thrilling.
Santa Clauses in streets shake their heads.
Children go running to them for their tweeds.
Their coy faces wish happiness.
They are live toys look such curios.
The last seven days of the year.
Every soul regales in revelry without any fear.

. . . .

(138)

MERRY CHRISTMAS TO ALL...

....

MERRY CHRISTMAS, MERRY
CHRISTMAS wishes to all.
In the lap of chilling December comes flowing in regale.
The beautiful day when the world
goes to moods of happiness.
Peace, prosperity & enlightenment come
to the world with pleasantries.
The SANTA CLAUSE.
Alight at home and roam in the streets.
Distribute happiness with a handshake,
Whoever comes?
Not only Christians but the other religions join too.
Assemble at the churches, temples
for praying peace in to woo.
Feelings of fraternity flow in abundance.
Peace should no more be a hindrance.
The poor to rich let everybody rejoice.
Cakes to pastries be in every mouth.
The moment is all that matters for both.
Men, women & children rush for picnicking.
Enjoy the day to the full brim with
beautiful happy glowing.

....

(139)

Feelings of Happiness...

Happiness is a great feeling,
Where the mind & soul go reeling,
Loss the feet from the ground,
Soul feel ecstatic goes in round,
The moment such rare,
Comes always with a feel & glare,
The galaxy of relatives in your doorstep,
When you share & distribute your happy steps,
Sons, daughters, parents, aunts & aunties,
Come home with sweet tooty-fruities,
Eat & revel go merry making,
It's yearend time go celebrating,
Amidst such fun your offspring gets engaged,
Happiness doubles up the family feels enchanted,
The moods go dancing and singing,
Real time for family to celebrate and go dancing.
Beautiful moments &feelings,
Grab the soul's in full moody mimicries,

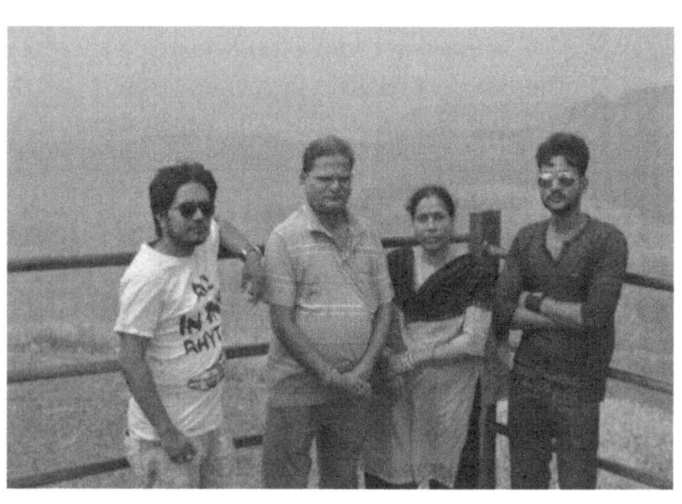

(140)

Off springs...

Off springs,
The real rings,
In your life when they arrive,
Have shortage of time still thrive,
The jerks & springs,
That rolls to throw you in rings,
You need to hang on,
Keep life busy to hold on,
Life a beautiful dream,
Takes out your pain in true realm,
Grow them educate them,
Give company to them,
Take care of them,
Live with them,
Love them,
Life is a long journey,
Love & time are full of honey.
Take the honey,
Take the nectar,
Be the rector...

(141)

My Sweet Granny....

....

Granny's smiles,
Always riles,
Her million dollar smiles,
Bring so much happiness,
She is the nanny,
Speaks only honey,
The grandchildren her world,
She relishes between them behold,
Look at her face,
The whole life stories wrinkles the trace,
The beautiful smile makes heart race,
She is our nanny in septuagenarian,
Memories unfold the awesome ton,
Her blessings open the façade,
The doors of smiles open ajar with arcade,
Her spectacles make her trail,
Her silver grey hairs are assets in her frail,
Failing to recognize faces today,
Unless seen from a close angle during the day,
She is beautiful & happy in her sojourn,
Life the great step she walked & run,

....

(142)

The Song of the Year End...

. . . .

Some untold feelings of happiness in the heart,
The year is about to end the word to breathe last,
Just seventy two hours of the clock to tick,
The hearts are racing in speed brake neck,
Churches to temples all are glittering,
With light of the year breathing in flattering,
Where ever eye goes all packed with people,
Making merry enjoying the leaving year in true purple,
The old order change giving place to the new,
The shrill voice of the new born is just going to renew,
Chilling cold to snows covering the ground,
People are flocking to fire woods for going around,
Heat of the sun gives warmth to the skin,
The body warms up with the heart akin,
Just count the happenings & important events of the year,

When the year leaves its scalps bid
a true farewell with cheer,
American to Indian to the British
along with the entire universe,
The entire continents in ecstasy &
awesome moods of rejoice.
The year is sleeping under the cover of the thick blanket,
To save its skin from the chilling weathers basket,
New Year...New Year... New Year the music in every voice,
Sings the choir from youth to old in true rehearses...

....

(143)

Tear' s of the centuries...

....

The tear drops that fell a century back,
Still bleeds heart with the hack,
For a moment soul travels the century back,
To catch a glimpse of the tear that's shelved in the rack,
The prying eyes of beloved's mom,
Never allowed us to even cry aplomb,
Her roving eyes were more fixed on the tomb,
Wherever we hide she found us bomb,
Every passing day made us miserable,
Our aches in the hearts cried pitiable,
The Achilles hills cried with sounds feeble,
Had no way out but to behave humble,
Finally one day she put the guillotine on relation,
Chopped the relation into pieces in total abnegation,
Gasping in utter frustration,
To catch a last glimpse before final repudiation.
The century old story hunts like a ghost,
Never again dared to be my host,
In the lap of eternity that we were lost,
To remember relation that never could last.

....

(144)

Renewed Faith..

....

Time has no death,
Time just renews faith,
With every beat of the pulse,
Life writes wonderful tales,
Everyone here is mortal,
But time is just immortal,
Walking running sleeping,
Since time started growing,
All living creatures are her children,
Playing the game of life in her yard often,
The players just forget the count,
But time never forgets to discount,
When a flower lives just for day,
A tree lives how long none can say,
But every one dies at the end of the day.
But time never dies,
Time always saves beautiful memories...
The year prepares to leave,
The New Year comes alive,
Time is the groom,
The new bride of time is just welcome...

....

2015

(145)

The Happenings...

The waiting still,
Keeps me waiting.
Soul packed with anxiety,
Waiting with patience and punctuality.
After placing the peace on the altar,
Leave it to destiny to decide the category of star.
Whether one star or five star,
What is it all that matter.
The rating a good judgement,
Leaves me to suffer the indictment.
When thoughts do not capture,
Heart & mind bleeds with desire.
The desire to write a creative piece,
To quench the waiting soul,
Reader's to rest in peace.
The old year leaves it's scalp,
The New Year's Eve at every door step.

(146)

The New Year Day..

....

The sky is overcast,
The weather wearing a mast,
Depressed look with the sky fully overcast,
As if the hangovers of the year bygone,
Will fall loose with tears of the heaven,
The entire atmosphere is just sober,
Washed with the drizzling sprinkler,
The atmosphere in moods of raining cool,
The year is catching up with moods to drool,
Everyone running for little shelter,
For saving the self from the rough weather,
The New Year begins with an overhaul,
Washing the earth, trees to people,
A welcome sign of the divine planning,
The year to be peaceful & prosperous
with good beginning...

....

(147)

Oracles of the Dreamland ...

. . . .

Beauty & Intelligence,
Feel their presence,
Work miracle,
Like the oracle,
A beautiful woman,
Best companion of man,
The man's mind,
She always binds,
Know no limits,
The geography of quests,
Roaming in mental planes,
Use the beautiful brains,
Beautiful fragrant bodies,
Craving for more of discoveries,

. . . .

(148)

The Silver linings..

....

Between the silver linings,
The domes of fortune,
The silver lining solicits open,
All eyes drawn attracted,
Desires of mind playing distracted,
When the veil of glass,
Divides the figurine lass,
The thin transparency in between,
The sounds of the pulse the point of break even,
Beating hum drum,
Only if the beloved could feel with her palm,
The palm can feel the beautiful music,
The heart plays sounding like a rustic,
When palms go locking into each other,
Soul's lost in mesmerism celebrate happier...
In life love is sheer fortune,
Be with the moment never to be forgotten

....

(149)

The Romancing Mind..

. . . .

The mind romances,
The soul in beautiful nuances,
Surrenders to the mind's dictates,
The mind in love with soul's ecstasies,
Nature's hidden manners,
Dormant invisible desires,
Zooming in the soul's corridors,
The souls' quest is hidden treasures,
Sink in the fathomless depths,

. . . .

(150)

In the Land of Snow Dust...

....

In the land of snow dust,
The couples in unique post.
Hug for little warmth,
Body is cold but heart's in trust.
Made for each other,
The nature & ambience a just welcome with their furs.
The soul connects,
What the world sees let none dissect.
This is life.
Such rare moments need a treat with the life.
The soul needs to leave its dusts,
The body needs to leave its frosts.

....

(151)

The Cracks in Relationship...

. . . .

The cracks in relationship,
Takes no name of a patch up.
Words of mouth fired like arrows,
Battered the relation to death with wordy blows.
The blows & punches leave a wound,
A bruised & battered relationship on the ground.
Yesterday's heart throb's behaving like stranger,
Turned rejected faces wounding the heart further.
Misunderstandings take no name of ending,
Salt to sour add up worse in the making.
The ravaged bruises take no name of healing,
Only hatred & dejected moments keep rolling.
The rings of love repudiated to destiny,
Empty-ness only cry at the beloved's plight of mutiny.
The winds of mutiny that blown up devastating,
The soul swelling with tear's frustrating.
Look at the villains, who played the game foolish,
Cracks take time to heal up but never finish.
The foul games played since time immemorial,
Romeo & Juliet to Heer & Ranjha all suffered it mortal...

. . . .

(152)

The Selfish World...

A selfish world,
Nobody is yours even if you cried.
All false pretentions,
Surround the intentions.
Fake identities,
Every moment you live in falsities.
People say, say the truth,
Even sages here do not utter truth.
Everyone says truth that suits,
Intentionally twisting the wits.
Be at your wits end,
You always have to bend.
This is life which always plays gimmicks,
Surprises in store for man to play the abuses.
Every man wears the attire of a gentleman,
The naked frame is never seen.
The attire itself is a false protection,
To hide his nudity and truths hidden.
The interior of man is full of lust,
Unless one clears them they just bust.
Man is slave of desires,
Fights to satisfy the lust coated with pleasures.

(153)

The Silent Face of turbulence..

....

The turbulence is over,
The tides that hurriedly arrived at my shore,
Wrought the devastation,
The sandy beach wore a look of desertion,
To assuage the loss,
To pacify the anguish,
To calm the rough tides,
The sea had to surrender,
Tranquil itself for better atmosphere,
The gravity had to bow down,
The seeds of peace sown,
Life was to be restored to normalcy,
The atmosphere begged for clemency,
Patience was the lighthouse,
That stood a mute spectator to douse,
When you visit next visit the light house,
To open the page wrought on its silent face,

....

(154)

When the World would learn Love...

Love is the word that binds us.
War is the word that grinds us.
It is always better to be bound.
Than get chased like a blood hound.
Love is the essence of life,
War is always ridden with strife.
Why not the world follows one word.
Love each other than using the sword.
The trigger hunting should vanish,
Men & women should have a lovely wish.
Always connect the beautiful minds,
Into peaceful sojourns of lovely winds.

(155)

The Pre-natal Connections...

....

Occupied prior to my existence,
Did not know my state of trance.
Inside the mother's womb,
The seedling was like a pulp.
In just nine months it grows in shape,
To be delivered to the world outside.
Floating inside the cell of fluid.
The child was just delivered,
Mother's love for the new born grows doubled.
Never wanting to part the child for a moment,
Mother wanted to hold the child tight.
Hug the child with godly kiss of love for the new born,
Her milk just enough to silence the baby born.
The child clung to them sucking all the nectar from mom,
The baby just peeing, wetting & passing on the mom,
No complain from the child's mom.
Just sacred waters for her,
Sacred touch for her,
The smells were eternally fragrant to her,
A sacred unique bond that meant life to her.
Life to her, life for her, life of her.

....

(156)

The Empty Chest...

....

When you open the chest,
Only the remains stay in no's & nots,
When the chest is empty,
Only void & vacuum reigns pretty,
The remains only give so much pain,
The soul cries & bleeds insane,
Life becomes sheer nuisance,
A matter of total abnegation & annoyance,
Lifeless puppets dance to the strings,
The chest has no treasures,
Even with keys,

....

(157)

Seven poets from the oasis

A jewel for the seven in the crown,
For a poet a beautiful gown.
The poetic acumen,
Comes with regimen.
The heart gets filled,
More of poems will be spilled.
Poetic spills enthralling the heart,
Universe knows the poet's faith.
An award a crown in the desert,
The poet feels with pride its worth.
The might of his pen,
Dressed with drunken wisdom & acumen.
Once again the desert blooms,
The storms of happiness start to loom,
The poet's foot in mouth.
In a desert an oasis the only truth.

(158)

The Angry River.

....

The river was angry,
The fathomless depth was hungry.
When four friends reached the river,
The river behaved like a sweet sixteen lover.
All the four jumped into the water,
In moments none could be traced beyond water.
The crowd swells in minutes,
The rescuers to the police.
Only dead bodies were recovered from the hungry river,
The river was flowing unchallenged
without any remorse in its behavior.
Tear's swelled to form a river,
But no one listened the prayer.
Life one's gone never recover.
There was a prayer in the college hall,
All friends to foes cried for the pal.
Gloom ruled the atmosphere,
Candle lights were burn in memoir.
A befitting tribute to the lost souls,
In their last journey to be remembered.

....

(159)

The False Shadows of Life...

....

My shadows of life chase me,
My shadows of life betray me,
At times when I try to overpower them,
They run away from my aim,
At times when I run to capture them,
The mirage hunt ends in mayhem,
Play the game of touch & vanish,
In the twinkle of my eyes the lashes,
The la belle dame game of finish,
Catch them alive is a dream come true,
Catch them dead is a mirage in blue...
Tired after a hectic chase,
Surrender to the gimmick losing my face

....

(160)

The Cardinal Truth...

....

Death is cardinal truth,
It keeps one waiting since birth.
Like a dry leaf falling every morning,
Life would desert the body keeping everyone in mourning.
The family's loss,
Death the cruel boss.
One soul leaves,
One enters.
The cardinal truth of life & death,
A thin line divides life from death.
The body slept several nights,
But one final sleep takes all his rights.
The soul mingles into the space's vastness,
Chasing life for little space.

....

(161)

The Gale that blew...

It was a gale that blew,
In the winds everything flew.
Now that everything is gone,
No more sit under the lamp post and mourn.
Time, life & fortune,
When all betray everything looks so torn.
The last straw of life,
Now sinks into the abysmal depth of rife.
From the abyss how to arise,
Even if things happen it will be no surprise.
Walk those steps of life,
Without remorse or strife.
From the eternal slumber,
No one wakes up ever.

(162)

Space for breathe....

....

The flavor of green,
From tea to nature's green.
A wonderful flavor filters the mind,
Filters the ambient moods & the wind.
The swift morning breeze passes with moods,
Catching up with the moods of the poets to brood.
Brood over word after word,
To compose a green poem for the world.
Too much of everything is bad,
The inhabitants are too hard.
Their only passion is destroy the green,
Cut the trees around turn the earth into an oven.
The soil is given a dressing with cement,
Concrete plantations come up soaring without any lament.
Let the world realize its mistakes,
Never venture to repeat them just for stakes.
No sooner the universe turn to a heat chamber,
Life gasping for little fresh air.
No one looks serious,
Let the universe go the way ferocious.
One day the number of vehicles would be more than man,
Forget about the animals that helplessly die in the run.
Man never learns unless the fury of nature shows its teeth,
Laughing at man's false ego for breathe.

....

(163)

Sipping the Nectar.

....

Sipping the nectar in slow pace,
Moods catching up for poetic space.
The poetic lines taking birth,
The poet in labor pain scribing bath.
The songs of labor pain breaking the path,
The limbs of the fetus arrive fast.
The placental connect keeps calling,
The howling baby continues yelling.
Survival of the fittest,
Music keeps playing in the beat.
The child is hungry for food,
The nature of mother provide the feed.
Lulling the child into lap of her natural amber,
The child lost into evanescent slumber.
The mother rhyming lullabies to nurture.

....

(164)

Beaten by the lover...

....

The beloved's lips only locks when beaten by the lover,
In the still waters of the pond the human mind ponders.
Lips of beloved wink the wave to wonder,
One losses the self when sensuous
desires create ripples in yonder.
The floating algae only spread green to
the pond sinking the pond's water,
But the beloved's lips only locks when beaten by the lover.

....

(165)

Obsession in Plight...

Most times wrong at times right,
That is the human obsession in plight.
Thoughts most times do not match the words,
Words most times do not match thoughts.
A great divide to languish,
Between the heart & soul both such fake & temporal,
While one is eternal the other ephemeral.
When one does not know destinations,
One languishes between the if's & but's of aspirations.
Endless human desires,
When one want gets satisfied another in it's space.
Man in his mundanely aspirations at times turns blind,
Who can stop the unending aspirations of the mind?

(166)

The Act of Life...

....

Life is a big drama,
Acts enacted in beautiful panorama.
Every man for that sake is a supreme actor,
Turning acts with finish with super man's factor.
Look at a road side beggar,
A live in actor.
Superb skills of acting for stomach,
The alms begged for stomach.
The beggar's hut no less than a palace,
The family enjoys real happiness.
Year after year a new born fills up the little space,
No space for little loneliness.
Often a rebel is born there,
Inheriting poverty here.
In such hand to mouth situations,
The beggar a routine practitioner to his professions.
Survive or perish becomes his coin for life,
The beggar to superstars everyone live a life.
Each lives according to his own,
No one's concern to frown.

The afterlife lessons are truly hard,
To fill the stomach's gap,
Animal to man to every living creature have a match.
A beggar or superstar.
Both imitates each other in their climax,
For one it is a compulsion,
The other a passion by choice.
Both eke out a living,
One whose bowl is empty,
The other has space to amass fortune's humpty dumpty.
Everyone born with an invisible bowl in hand,
Eke out a living or die of hunger with tied hands.

. . . .

(167)

Feel the song....

When the deafening voice cried,
None listened.
The soul only feels the pangs,
The mind feels the bangs.
When one sings with a deafening voice,
It is a soulful song sung with remorse.
The melody mellifluously passes,
The soul helplessly watches oblivious.
Transcendence surrounds,
Bliss truly abounds.
The voice is stifled,
A humming voice riddled.
The fusion of silence,
A deafening voice.
Only the singer can listen,
Feel the song's pulse beaten.

(168)

The Paper Boat...

. . . .

When rains came during childhood,
In one corner of the verandah I stood.
Sailed the paper boats one after the other,
The boats sailed a while in the rain water.
Heaven's heaved a sigh of relief,
My bewildering soul waited,
For another rainy day of if's & but's.
Ecstasy swelling in my little heart,
Treasured in memory till I became an adult.

. . . .

(169)

A Tiny Spark by Tiny Hands...

Setting fire to the heap of straw,
We trinity set fire to the heap.
Infancy in aggression,
Setting fire to the heap in procession.
Flames were engulfing the atmosphere,
The towering inferno set the whole village ablaze,
A tiny spark by tiny hands made the raze.
The teacher to elders all aghast,
At the childish act,
Slaps fell one over the other,
The trinity crying aloud tearing the skies ether.
.That was childhood,
That had no hood.

(170)

The Child in me always lives...

. . . .

If again my dad gives me a catapult,
That flies me to the childhood from adult.
Like a kite I would fly only to be on
the blue sky's huge space,
Take the catapult and shoot the monkeys
that hide in the mango groves.
The child in me always lives.

. . . .

(171)

The Campfire & the Romance...

The campfire & romance,
Burns the logs & the sighing bodies.
The flames of passion,
With the flames of the fire atone.
Atone the passions,
Set the logs into fire,
When two soul's meet at the campfire.
One ignites the logs,
The other the passions.
Under the blankets wrapped,
The body's triggers fully charged.
A just touch tingles,
The mouth waters to mingle.

(172)

The Waiving hands

....

When her hands just went waving,
My waiting soul passionately goes flying,
The whole world appeared green,
With one single trigger the soul felt the unseen,
Anxiously waiting for the moment,
In adolescence for two dying souls
it was a beautiful foment,
A smile from the beloved returned with double payment,
That pacified the body & mind of the soul in joint...
Life s' worth felt even without a penny in the pocket,

....

(173)

The Serene Dawn.

....

The glistening dew droplets,
Sliding aplomb on the green grass.
The dawn is just waking up from slumber,
Moods of the dawn fast catching up with the amber.
The tiny bulbs holding gravity,
The bulb attracts the dawn's beautiful sensitivity.
Creating a fusion of the nature's surprises,
The dawn's tender feelings,
Give feelings of freshness.
The green grass,
Wearing a carpet of pearl on its green surface.
The mesmeric of nature for the vision to wonder,
The soul feels drunk with the nature.
The green carpets give feelings of sheer oblivion,
Mission of life accomplished with the serene vision.

....

(174)

When Bliss visits Transcendence

....

What the mind cooks,
The recipes given in the books.
The mind relishes the hooks,
The soul bickers in murmuring the lines.
The whispers discuss the feelings,
Between solitudes,
Books keep the soul busy inventing new altitudes.
Books are life's best friends,
The pages do not rest as one unfolds.
Every day a new bud blooms in the garden of books,
The reader to writer everyone engrossed
in the orchard of words.
Nurturing the buds to grow in the hearts,
The words only whisper more of space.
For the soul to take a dip in the fathomless embrace,
The closed door of the cocoon opens in faith.
Time forgets its nature sinking deep into the path,
Bliss visits transcendence.
The soul smells the abundance,
Lost in deep fragrance.

....

(175)

The Eternal Bed of Silence

....

The Desert sleeps in silence,
Like a beautiful mermaid with the dunes.
Her serene looks and the footsteps,
Breaking her silence the camels walks.
With the Bedouins eking out a livelihood from the deserts,
The oasis a mirage in the deserts lengthy sands.
None can measure the gravity of silence.
The desert meditates like a monk,
From time immemorial in silent wink....

....

(176)

Memories on the banks of time...

....

The Yesterday is a just memory.
What happened yesterday?
Appears like a myth today.
Even the memory is fresh,
But things once gone carry no trace.
Whatever is encrypted in memory?
Remains a shrouded mystery.
Unless one converts them to words,
No way there to prove the deeds.
Only glimpses of such memories,
Hurt & hunt the mind like treasuries.
Neither one can reject them,
Nor can repudiate them,
Birth till death the real mayhem.

....

(177)

A Sunday today

....

On my roof top today,
An evening on a Sun day.
The night wearing a darker robe,
The sky looks dense black the darker garb,
The stars twinkling the night,
Shining the carpet with starry night.
The eyes fail to reach,
The vision remains fixed for preach.
The great curtain that divided the day from the night,
Continues to drop without any fright.
The universe belongs to me amidst too much priority,
Wait till the morning for sun light.

....

(178)

Quake plays havoc

. . . .

When quake hits,
Quake hit people,
Quake hit land,
Buildings to structures falling like cards.
With one shake of the earth's crust,
The colossal loss,
Loss of human life,
Loss of flora, fauna.
Massive pain for the humans,
Some one's near,
Someone's dear.
The quake had no choice,
Whoever came its way lost his ways.

. . . .

(179)

The Sweated Drops...

....

The Glistening Dimples.
Had blood & sweat,
On its spread.
Love stood in silence,
The golden drops fell from the eyes.
Tearing my heart into pieces.
Crying with each falling drop,
Feelings reasoned for heart stop.
The rebukes of the peers fell in deaf ears,
When the hearts melt none can put stoppers.
When the ice melts it turns into water.
When you crucify love tears to blood fall,
The cries are unheard love stands tall.
In solitude lovers behave like angel.
Watching the guillotines sharp razor's
hanging over the head,
Love was beheaded but silence stood,
The glistening dimples had blood & sweat on its spread,
The cross stood mute watching the soul's butchered.

....

(180)

Waiting for None

....

Time & Tide wait for none.
Time does not halt,
Tides do not wait.
The moving hand rounds,
The vast space by leaps & bounds.
Every minute a pulse fails,
Every second one new soul arrives.
Between Life & Death,
A thin invisible line,
The unseen & the seen,
What is seen?
At times goes unseen,
What is unseen?
Is a mystery never seen?

....

(181)

Ignorant Manners...

....

When the mother earth cracked,
Heaves & cries of the cracks were heard,
Blood struck bodies lye on the road,
By the action everyone is stunned,
Nature strikes its cruelty,
In unwanted manners of hurt,
Life to non-life all run for little open space for,
Even the open space has no space to offer,
You run for shelter elsewhere,
There is no space here,
You better find shelter elsewhere,
Else the earth will grasp under its care,

....

(182)

Jubilees...

....

Life's jubilees...
Twenty five beautiful years,
So much happiness amidst tears,
Glimpses of memories,
A beautiful treasury,
The wealth of love,
Hides in the locker of the beloved's grove,

....

(183)

Calamity jolts

....

When the Earth takes a turn,
So many come under it so many mourn.
One shakes of the earth's crust,
The bones of the earth break the trust.
Ancient monuments & temples to tombs collapse,
Underneath the debris lye the dying souls.
Above the earth bereaved families.
The river of sorrow flows.
Natures' fury & wrath jolts with blows.

....

(184)

The Eternal Thirst

Quenching the thirst.
Drenched up trusts,
Hooked up throttles,
All dance there,
In the huge amphitheater,
The rains gone,
The wind touching my bones,
Searching the moment,
For one more event.

(185)

The Ultimate Ironies

....

The Stomach an eternal criminal,
The food chain alive since time immemorial.
A beautiful fish in devour,
Beautiful beaks of the heron in hunger.
The physical need,
The mental greed.
Stomach needs two seeds,
Save the physical body.
Supplement the mental body,
One is the body's greed,
The other is lust indeed.
Pulverizing the human mind,
Every moment the mind takes a grind.
Life needs food,
Life needs blood.
Love needs food,
Love needs blood.
The food & blood twin make the livelihood.
Animal to man,
Flora & fauna,
No one escapes the food chain.

....

(186)

The Tragic Monument... [Dharara]

....

Everything gone in moments,
When mother earth changed her tectonic plates.
All the visitors to watching men,
Everyone in the graveyard under the minaret's den,
When the minaret crumbled into pieces,
Everything life to non-life turned into ashes.
Tragedy struck onlookers,
Ran helter-skelter for open space,
The mother had already opened its face.
One after the other fell into its wells.
The mother earth at times so magnanimous.
Accepting the terror stricken souls,
The survivors abdicate homes,
Everything turned turtle.
Homes no more remained homes.

....

The Monument Dharara, Nepal could not withstand the shock of the Earthquake that blew it into pieces

(187)

A Gun in the mouth

....

The Blindness.
Putting a gun in mouth,
You said leave her,
I said,
I would not,
You better fire.
The moment you fired me to death,
My beloved breathe her last.

....

(188)

Hiding in disguise

Every living creature in guise,
Thou presence a real surprise.
Male to female all thou prize,
Every morning the sun rises.
Since time immemorial reality surprises,
When the sun sets in the evening.
The stars surprise with their twinkling,
The crescent arc comes smiling.
Wishes drill holes in the opposites,
The Seeds nurtured by the opposites.
When they incubate the seeds for germination,
The tender leaf to palm a sheer inspiration.
Inspiration for life to sprout,
Fill up the gaps of the universe with an imprint.
God's divine ordination,
Extremely engrossed fathomless coordination.
Round the clock the unseen hand shouts for action,
Everything such preordained,
Not a leaf moves without consent in the domain.
The thin veil of disguise,
An unseen enterprise.
Invisible to the naked eye,
Soul of which lives inside.

(189)

The Day leaves for the Night

....

When a tired day leaves for the night,
The sun starts setting in the west,
The evening star & the galaxies come to greet.
The day forgets its existence,
In the milieu of galaxy's presence.
The night lulls the day to sleep,
With the cool moon beams the stars peep.
The night covers itself with the starry jacket,
The huge carpet hiding the Night's
queen in the dark pocket.
Rolling in the bed of the slumber,
Dreaming the graceful amber.
Day waking at the dawn leaving the night.
The morning birds singing alarm,
For the day to wake up from the night's fairy arm.
The bliss full moods of the dawn,
Welcome calmness to the horizon
Welcoming everyone to rehearse the acts again,
Same rituals repeated at the dawn.
Dawn till dusk the day delves into silent action.

....

(190)

In the Fathomless Embrace

....

When in deep embrace,
Both forgot grace.
Both fought the battle,
Both needing to settle.
Invasion of the mind,
Happens to bind.
Soul's quest,
The soul knows best.
The happy sojourn,
Ends in happy runs.
Emotions fully charged,
Untold feelings barged.

....

(191)

Thoughts of you

I never thought so much about you,
In my solitudes time never allowed me to meet you,
The heart's image was always flashing before eyes,
No mirror to see the reflective cease,
Water of the oceans kept me thirsty,
The salt waters of the ocean can't satiate.
My lone-self remained forever thirsty,
When I tried to console you,
You never understood,
Left me alone to be misunderstood.

(192)

The catapult of Love

. . . .

When you borrowed my books,
My heart was hooked by your looks.
The catapult of love fires,
It injures none but the lover's ire.
You left a dry leaf inside the pages,
I treasured the leaf in my soul's cages.
Caressing the tender leaves,
Infusing life into it through the heaves.
You underlined some lines,
In my ignorance I mugged up all line by line.
Reciting the lines again & again,
Till my pulse danced to the tune.
Feelings of love for a lover,
Nothing less than the pearl oyster.
Treasured between the cocoons,
The pearl of love signs like a beacon,

. . . .

(193)

Soul in Ransom

Chasing a mad passion,
Do not know the reason.
Why thoughts take birth?
Why the mind thinks aftermath?
Why the mind scribbles them into a language,
Fellow friends pour compliments of assuage.
Wait in vein,
Near the lamp post at the lane.
Mutely stand looking at the skies,
Stars test your patience while the brain fries.
Who will come?
To the emotion dome.
The emotion a state of mind,
Keep waiting for the friend?
Dry leaves amass on the street,
Silently falling on to the earth's feet.
The mother's great heart,
Absorbs every odd,
Even dirt to be good.
Chasing a mad passion,
Mind takes the soul to ransom,

(194)

Take Life Easy

. . . .

The flames leave the cauldron black,
Wishes are not horses face the abrupt hack.
The journey full of thorns,
The thorns prick throughout pushing the horns.
Soft pedaling never pays,
Take life easy life pays.
The fortunes of life never amass,
All vanish in the flames in one hash.
Beautiful thoughts born in moments,
Reading beautiful poetic thoughts.

. . . .

(195)

Blind Alibis

....

Beauty & Woman
Wild nature of man.
Chasing the beautiful woman,
Wonders man.
Open or close everyone,
Attracted to the magic woman.
Look at the soft petals,
Look at the tender looks.
Look at the sweet voice,
Look at the sweetness.
All mesmerize & impress,
She is the tigress.
She the Goddess,
The opposite sex.
Man's greatest weakness,
Man's Achilles hill, satire & passionate choice.
Every man silently wishes to possess,
The honey bee that she is.
One spoonful of the honey enough to hypnotize,
Lifelong bickering of the restless soul.
God's magic gift for man to feel.
A captive mine of love in duress.

....

(196)

The Fragrant Night Queen

The fragrant night queen,
Spraying the pungent fragrance fine.
The moonlit night's décor,
The soul thanks the maker.
The amber's broad chests,
Planets shining with presence.
The nocturnal creatures,
The nocturnal desires.
Assemble to exhibit the image,
The queen of ambience opens her foliage.
Romantic expression on every face,
No place to hide the grace.
Caught by the wrong foot,
The culprit's foot in mouth.
Looting the cleavages,
Secrecies of the foliage.
The fragrance looting the soul's treasuries,

(197)

The Magic of Vocabulary

....

Vocabulary is like a constable trafficking,
Words ought to know the signals well before flickering.
It is like a flickering candle,
When the light ends you are packed in bundle.
Go to heaven or go to hell,
The devil goes ringing the bell.
Your vocabulary is an expired product,
All your wrong actions will face deduct.
Just choose the words right,
Be precise in your concept & write.
Unless you follow the right sequence,
All your efforts ruining the defense.
Better be apt,
Always maintain the heart,
Choose the right words never dirt.
Thoughts must have a conceptual meaning,
Before words conceive just tune the feeling.

....

(198)

Hundreds of years after

....

Hundreds of years after,
You will find from me the same answer.
Even if you dig the graves,
Innocence will be written large on my face.
I am the same me,
Whether you check me alive or my mummy.
Your beautiful face,
Famous for its vanity & egos.
Preferred severing in life,
Rejecting the relationship to rot in rife.
The wordy duel,
Adds spice to the fuel.
Our detractors make merry & regale.
Your mom & my dad,
The obstacles posed very hard.
Neither could we open our mouth,
To suffer the slitting of relation by throat.

Throttled by the neck,
Worse than the butcher's hack.
Our cries fell in deaf ears,
Even if it was brutal & tortuous.
But no blood spilled on roads,
Souls torn into pieces.
Throttled by the neck for a happy death,
Everyone behaved merciless.

....

(199)

Soulful Renditions

. . . .

Classical music concert,
The lady flutist.
The male saxophonist,
The strings of the satirist.
The brother's chanting the classic lines,
Purifying the soul's mesmerizing mines.
The listener's soul in paradise,
What is sung, what is played by the artists?
The accompanying tabla player's finger beats,
All enchanting the soul to oblivion,
The fountain of bliss in fusion.
The awestruck audience,
Rapt attention to each tune.
To each thread fine.
Opulence in realism,
The soul baths in surrealism.
Surreal feelings descend,
The soul's backyard full of blend.
Blending serenity,
Infinity to divinity.
Soul in transcendence,
Nothing but the fathomless.

. . . .

(200)

Faith

Before the temple yard,
Pigeons livelihood.
The human slavery,
A blind signatory.
Feed the parrots,
Boon for seven life's sought,
Blind signatory to the faith.
A good deed in truth,
The love for pigeons.
An ancient thought.
Indian homes,
Love the pigeons dome.
Feeding pigeons for boon,
From wealth to moon,
Full of fortune.
What not arrives?
The good deed drives.
Homes fortune flowers,
God's blessings pour.

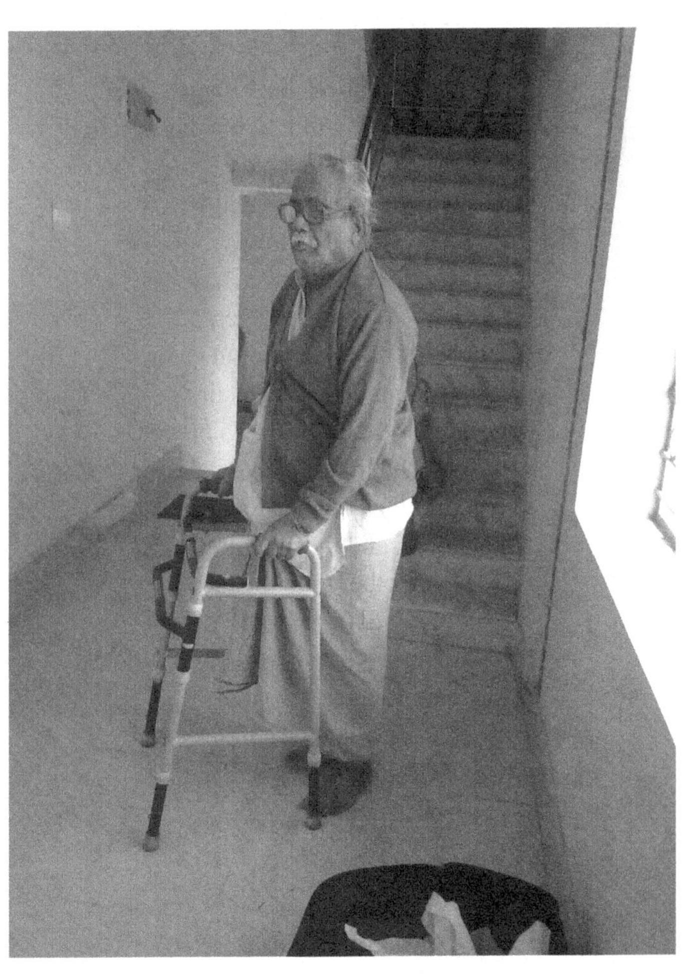

(201)

The Grand Old Man

The Old man loves the village,
The house built by him of his days.
The village temple,
His passion for life in ample.
The green pastures,
To the village river.
Revered by the villager,
His age a testimony of the survivor.
The old man's wheel chair,
Moves temple ward for God's prayer.
The Old man's walker,
Help him the distance to cover.
His fat body and the huge stature,
He is none other than the father.
Many odds to even,
Countless good deeds,
Committed by for good.
Now in old age remains a milestone,
Long live! Long live! Old man,
We stand by you.

(202)

The Astral Plains

. . . .

The placental connect keeps calling,
Love to be in the mother's wombs,
Love the connect that fed me ambrosia,
Love the connect that drank me the nectar,
Love the beats that played in my mother's tunes,
Lulling me to sleep in the lap of wombs,
I regret at existence today,
Why! Mom you brought me to the material world of today,
Beseech the astral plains that sheltered me in your wombs,
Today I run amok hate the satires of life,
Life's false mirages cheat me now & then,
Find no place for myself in this mundanely universe,
The womb of yours keeps me calling for a comeback,
I love to be there live in your shadows,
Life a false affair of deserted meadows.

. . . .

(203)

Symbolism in peace

At a confluence,
Five senses,
Five elements,
Truly make a beautiful sense,
Life without the five senses,
Life without the five elements,
Meaningless,
The five senses,
Play their roles.
When they play together,
The laws of evolution cheer.
The five elements,
Play their roles,
Life's dreams accomplish,
Lest deserts of sands,
Space in astray,
The almighty's superb evolution,
A miniature of the mass in creation,
Ignorance is bliss,
Ignorance is just peace.

(204)

The Fisherman & The Sea...

The Fishermen,
And the sea,
The blue tides of the sea,
Amphibians to fish,
The little boat,
Carry the fishermen,
Sea ward,
With their fishing nets,
When the sun sets,
Golden rays set in,
Reflections ripple on the surface,
The wooden boat with fish load,
Sails shore bound for little space,
The sea inside is calm,
Serene & still,
The fishing boat's tarpaulin,
Obey the winds,
The little fins of hope,
Ferry fishermen home,
The lamp of lighthouse beacons,
Beacon lights of hope,
From the turbulent waters to the shore,
Silence for ever remembered.

Akshaya Kumar Das

(205)

The Footprints

....

The Footprints,
Still bore the imprints,
Time a silent witness,
Passed swiftly for ages,
The couples look at the traces,
Left on the bank of ages,
The sand particles washed,
Innumerable tides bashed,
Tides returned with a small trace,
The particle for consequence,
In love's chapter of memory,
Pictures after pictures a nostalgia & treasury,
The blinking eye lids only remembered the episodes,
The lighthouse was the mute witness,
The saga of love was written on the sands,
Tides always envied the stories written on the beds,
Shadows of the traces still survive,
The lover's locked in the memorial vibes,
The nuances & the melodies of love,
Lost in the steps of time & strings of hope,
Like tides the lovers revisited the shores,
Time & again caught in the crush,
The razor of time only tears,
The eyes only bleed drops of tears,

....

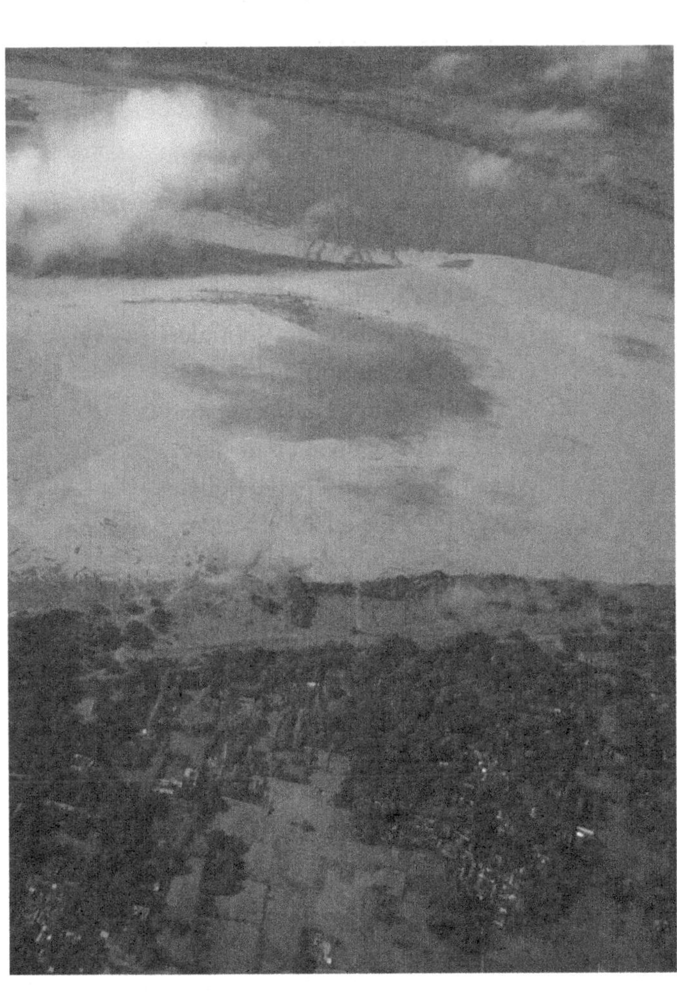

(206)

Nature's Mystic Smiles

The strand of wild grass,
An evanescent fragrance,
The uncombed morning hair,
Woken up from dawn's slumber for care;
The dawn & the beautiful face,
With radiant sun beams.
The dawn's abundant solitude,
Calmness to serenity in servitude.
The tender buds at sun's care,
Petals slowly open up to stare.
The honey bee kisses the pollens,
Carrying the dusts of pollen.
From one flower to another,
The bee to the butterfly nature's pollen carrier.
The pollination takes place,
Flowers bloom to fruit with awesome grace.
Nature's mystic smiles,
Fill the universe for miles & miles.

(207)

When She comes in my Dreams

When She comes in my dreams,
Polishes the flesh to bones with feelings.
The carnal desires,
Come like Safire.
Quests of my little island,
Roaming over its high land.
Lust full of senses,
Visit the pleasure fences.
Digging the trenches,
Beseech more of the embraces.
Remain hidden in the domes,
Hide between the cleavages.
The nature's carnal acts,
Performed with art.
The mind drinks the wine,
Bickers more of thine.
The volcano erupts,
Erupting the lava of thoughts.
The dormant volcano's ire,
Burns the passionate fire.
The body feels solace,
Hiding a blush red face.

(208)

The Caravan

Life is a caravan,
Journey in a universe full of men.
Regrets today for being born,
So much of struggle hidden.
Never was it known,
So much pleasure & so much pain.
One can't absorb but undone,
Pleasure follows pain.
Like two sides of the same coin.
Life follows death,
Death follows life.
Why one is born,
Where one dies,
None tell me yet mourn.
Some body tell me the truth,
Where life goes after death.
Why fall in love with life,
Why run after life.
When the ultimatum is death,
The caravan's journey end one day,
The earth never remembers the short stay.

(209)

The If's & But's

. . . .

Forgive me never,
Forget me not,
My love you never sought.
You walk yours,
I mine.
In crossroads
If ever we meet,
It is fine.
Do not say hello,
Just maintain low.
I will understand,
Silences best understand.
The paths are crossed,
Never could know when the road crossed.
Like an angel,
Roamed in my life.
Tearing the if's & but's of life.
In the if's & but's we are lost,
Memories chase most.
Shadows of life always cost,
Forgive me never,
Forget me not.

. . . .

(210)

Love You Mother

Love for the Mother,
Mother's love,
Thicker than the blood,
Pure than the nectar,
Mother's love is pure,
On mother's day,
Compliments to mothers,
For the best day,
Let children laugh with the beloved mother,
Let children cry for the beloved mother,
In the earth there is nothing greater than the Mother.
A Mother the mother of all creations,
Her renditions to hectic chores,
The child the only treasure in her books.

(211)

Cry the Beloved Country

Cry the beloved country,
Tears are never rivers to flow in bounty,
When tragedy strikes,
None come to rescue, but panic.
If only God alone can try,
Every odd ends in minutes, Why?
But who will whisper the message to god,
In God's universe is no one nearer to GOD?
Why give pleasure?
Why give pain?
When you have given so much, Why then?
Tragedies happen only in hell never in heaven.
The predicament hunts,
Plant to animal everyone feels the taunt,
Life & death are God's prerogative,
Let GOD understand tragedy's objective,
Let it not happen in hell alone,
Lest who will live here to atone.

(212)

Poets' World

When I dream of my poems,
Words put rhyme,
Rhyming in the mind is a happening,
Until the words are penned down,
Until the words take shape,
The poets mind goes restless,
The poets hunger shouts at his existence,
The poet runs for a loop,
End the affair with poetry,
Hating existence,
When thoughts do not process,
The process betrays,
The poet visits his subjects,
Morning to evening lost in their objects,
Nurturing them for sustenance,
Watering them with great patience.

(213)

Life of Woods

Every thought is not a seed,
Every thought does not breed,
Every embryo does not create,
But every poet always writes,
When thoughts loss their sight,
The poor poet runs for appetite,
Catch a glimpse of thought,
A small particle of sand to write,
When the particle gives a thought,
The poet steals the thought to write,
When mind fails to concentrate,
The heart of the poet is shattered to extent,
Thoughts do not roam in the vicinity,
Like vehicles running in the busy street,
Thoughts always move in camouflage,
The poet has to toil hard to choose,
Poet is never a dictionary,
But a poet writes always like a luminary,
Words infuse life into the milieu,
Words carve a niche truly in lieu,

(214)

An Ode to the Mother

How many years gone,
Mom since you left for heaven,
Glimpses of your face,
Appear before the house,
As the memories unfold,
Love is in behold,
We beseech your comeback,
Time only shows flash back,
In our silences your shadow alive,
Every now & then we have to believe,
Faith is great saying,
Accustomed to the sad loss keep praying,
In between the shadows we are caught,
Tears jerk up in the eyes corner,
Brother to sister we all cry for you with the father,
Our cries fall into deaf ears,
The well of our tears,
Drying up with fears,
Once the physical body is lost,
Next to impossible to get your trust,
Your pure love and affection,
Etched in our memory station,
Silently eschew the loss in total abnegation.

(215)

The Election Times

. . . .

As the four wheels arrive,
With a loudspeaker on its roof,
Run behind madly shouting with the speaker,
Zindabad, Zindabad, Zindabad slogans,
Filled the innocent ambience of the village,
The school boys winking through the windows,
Wishes taking part in the following,
The leader's election visit,
Cast your votes for his majesty,
All great promises made in amnesty,
From stomach full of food,
To all the good,
Including the dilapidated structure to the village road,
All get a facelift for the leader's arcade,
Promises fall from heaven like cascade,
Sweets in every mouth to sweetened words,
A leader who never did anything lived in words,
Tall promises reigned the atmosphere,
Smiles across all faces from old men to children,
The village will turn into a city arcade,
Water to electricity & what not,

. . . .

(216)

The Name of Break-up

That Name of Break up,
Takes No Name of a patch up,
The Name of love rots for life long,
The Name of love is hung,
Dyeing a death of banishment,
Love gives a cruel punishment,
Rest of the journey to begin,
Stay separated & lone,
Brooding over the relation,
Chase the soul life-long in utter abnegation,
Everything in the world appears false,
Interests in life's journey appear baseless,
Negative words only uttered from the mouth,
The lover's image in camouflage touches every truth,
A lone man in a vast desert's sandy patch,
Sporting white & black beards with scratch,
The wound of love never heals,
The pain is tortuous always kills,
Hard truths of life show their face,
Comes the face of first love,
why always.

(217)

The Smiling Lily's

. . . .

The Beautiful Lily,
Smiles from the pond daily,
The eyes just sink,
The heart just gets drunk,
The wandering soul behaves like a monk.
A captive image,
Stored in maize,
Words just puzzle,
The reader's dazzle,
Inquisitive mind,
Questions of unkind,
Ask the quizzing mind,
Why the lily blooms,
Why the sun radiate beams,
The lily wakes up from bud hood,
Blooms with its youthful petals proud,

. . . .

(218)

Navels

The Beauty in navels.
The artistic mind unravels,
The mystery hidden inside the navels,
The navel always attracts,
Even the blind too detracts,
Great saints fell victim,
To the navel's beautiful rim,
Navel is like an ornament,
Passion feels aroused with a dent,
The beautiful navels,
The roving eyes instantly smell.

(219)

The Centuries Old Shackles

Let the shackles of life unchain,
Let the bridles of love just open,
The centuries old shackles,
The centuries old bridles,
When loosen from pain,
Wait for the moon,
The shackles to open with pain,
The bridles to open with moan,
Freedom is my birthright,
From birth till death so much fight,
The chain of space locked tight,
Suffocating the space for a free breathe,
The pulse struggles to beat & breathe,

(220)

The Myriad Ways

Life's myriad ways,
Myriad desires
Drives life fight with wits end,
The wisdom of life,
Teach many stories,
The real stories are pranks,
Struggles to come out of situation,
Wisdom betrays time & again,
On the path of wisdom,
Who taught to trust?
Where from came the conscience to picture,
Always ask conscience before the venture,
Apply the conscience to every wrong act,
Pass the test before doing the act,
All a process of self-learning,
None to caution the truths burning,
Truths burn to ashes,
Ashes in the end leave no traces,
Search the footprints,
The fading imprints,
Nothing excavate,
Neither the ancient,
Nor the present.

(221)

Little Space

. . . .

The Leaves of Life amazing,
Look at the colors,
Look at the four letters,
Look at the hands that hold,
Life in its clutches,
The symbols of life,
Reflect fabulously,
Life in white letters,
Measures the space,
The huge blue space,
Life still struggles for little space.
Little space little breathing space.

. . . .

(222)

The Jungle Flower

....

She hides amidst the nature's green groves,
The green leafs and branches behind,
Beautifies the ambience with her beyond,
She is the love of my mind,
She truly shakes my soul to find,
The love of abundance flows with radiance,
The words of nature call me embrace,
Run for the beautiful face,
In the jungle's silence the touching race,
The jungle hides us inside her huge womb,
Caressing, fondling & fingers running the comb,
The saliva rollout with pleasure,
The drops of sweats with tear,
Wet flower & the aura,
She is none but the fragrant jungle flower,

....

(223)

The Effigy of my Soul....

When the fire burn,
Let me be burn,
The effigy of my soul burn,
Let the flames devour me,
Flesh to bone every part of me,
Let the ashes fly like wishes,
Mingle into the vast space,
Let the particles settle,
Shine alive like the flames,
Flora, fauna & man,
Whoever be it,
Does not remain,
The cycle ends,
One moment,
One minute,
One day,

Links left open,
Traces left behind,
Invisible links sustain,
Remain unseen,
The camouflage acts of the assassin,
Let the fire burn,
Let me be burn,
A last wish,
Let the flames devour me,

....

(224)

Doodle Do

With tears in my eyes,
Smiles on my lips,
Doles my heart,
Forgiving the nots,
Forgetting the nots,
Tears Miniature Rivers,
When in sorrow flow in abundance,
Smiles of oceans,
When swell tides touch you high,
Surf on the river,
Carrying the sorrow to the other end,
Surf on the oceans arc of tides,
Swim to the contents of the heart,
Till the tides defeat,
In some one's being born,
The tides of the heart's ocean,
Swell with high altitudes,
In some one's demise,
The river of tears flow abundant,
Till soul surrenders to the defeat,
Tear & smile duos,

Behave like twins,
When one cries,
The other envies,
Tear & smile two sides of the same coin,
With tears in eyes,
Crying your woes,
Release the blocks of emotions,
Release the woes,
Allow the ambers to absorb what goes,
Time is the true healer to heal your woes,
Laughter is the medium,
Medium of happiness,
Use laughter to overcome the woes,
Forgive the nots,
Forget the nots,
Doodle do the nots.

....

(225)

A Lover & the Lunatic

A Lover & the Lunatic,
One is blind another ascetic,
The lover is blind for love,
The lunatic's mind is skeptic,
The blind symphonies reeds,
The finger's nostalgic rhythmic beats,
Plays the tunes with season,
The lunatic's penchant for acumen,
Drawn passions with apt deadlines,
Schizophrenic tempests,
Blows like a flute in hurricane,
The ascetic's ropes,
Hold them for a flight of hopes.

(226)

The Eternal Swimmer

What is there?
In the moon light today,
Beheld in the ambient,
Moods just rejuvenate,
Soul's calling bells,
Pulls the triggers,
Oh! Moonlit Night,
Do not drift away,
To the cover of the clouds,
Remain forever there,
To place the mind without fear,
The eyes without tear,
Let the soul swim,
Till it feels the whim.

(227)

The Teeth of Time

. . . .

If it was prior,
Or the latter,
Which was better?
The romance before,
Or the romance later.
The mind always wanders,
Which was better?
Whether before,
Or after.
The soul always falters,
Feelings always vanish faster.
Feelings are dormant memories.
In need beseech both.
The before as well as the after.
The before had lot of imagination.
With the after everything is just gone.
The before is past.
The after is future.

The present always loiters.
Between the hope of future,
And the hopeless after.
The lost moments difficult to capture.
Vanishing like ether.
The fragrance sustains ether.
Seeking another before.
Seeking another after.

....

(228)

The Locks of summer

. . . .

Look at the flower,
Look at the summer.
The beautiful morning,
Locks of white leaves,
The colorless chlorophyll less.
Cascades of nature,
In love with the summer.
Before the eyes,
Eyes just behold.
Stop for a moment,
Look at the beauty.
Shot as a memento,
Nature's awesome present.
For the morning walkers,
To drink the beauty of dawn.
The furnace of heatwave.
The mind is brave.
Humid atmosphere,
Sweats trickling through the pores.

Wet the skin to glisten,
Smells of attraction in atmosphere.
With heart & mind,
Walk hand in gloves amidst the green.
Green pastures green trees,
Pregnant with white flowers.
Resembling nature's feminine locks,
The mind seeks to pluck,
Hands do not reach the trunk.

....

(229)

The Poem of Infinite ism

. . . .

If mandrake root was infinite,
If a falling star was infinite.
What an infinite ism,
Dreamt infinitesimal.
The mermaid is no realism,
The fathomless is pure surrealism,
In isms souls merge in,
The primordial existentialism,
The placental surrealism,
Feelings of infinity.
Hides somewhere in.
The inn or altar.
The mosque or the temple.
Where does the infinity exist.
Really exist.
The real existentialism,
Always eludes humanism.
Since time immemorial the philosophy of ism.

Just look at the prism,
If the maize is illusionism,
If the words are syllogism,
In so much falseness,
The fake universe,
Caught between the threads of Real & fake,
The struggle of universe at stake,
Time never dies,
Ism is cult of humanism,
Subjects to objects all live in a beautiful prism.

....

(230)

It's sheer Magic

. . . .

The magic hand,
Writes like a wand.
The magic hand,
Paints like a brand.
The magic voice,
Sings like a cuckoo.
The magic vision,
Doles with a reason.
The magic legs,
Walks the desert.
The magic minds,
Climbs the Everest.
The magic souls,
Flying to heaven.
The magic touches,
Heals the pain.
The magic sweeping,
Brooms the miseries.

The magic painting,
Soaks the soul in compassion,
The magic universe,
Must live in peace.
The magic of space,
Give the magic to the universe.
Fellow feelings,
A bouquet full of happiness.

....

(231)

The Ignorant Alibis

....

The alibi of ignorance,
When the flower spreads its fragrance,
Does not herself know meaning of essence,
The fragrance attracts every soul,
From moth to men every soul,
Visits the flower to discover.
The treasure,
Fragrance like ether,
Radiates in the atmosphere,
The dictionary of smell,
Opens the fragrant veil,
Soul to unravel,
Searches in the garden's vacant cradle.

....

(232)

The Axis of the Earth

....

The earth ceaselessly rotates,
Around the axis,
Since the birth of time,
None predicts when time was born,
The Rule of seasons,
In summers the pride of heat,
In rains the rains just swelling the rivers,
In autumn the autumnal show of festivals,
In winter the frozen souls,
Freezing in deeper Himalayas,
In spring the cuckoo,
The mesmerizing orchestra of the mango groves,
The ears soothing,
The eyes bow with devotion,
The mind sheltering in bliss,
Transcendental prides,
Egos washed,
Pride belongs to no one,

....

(233)

The Pride of Moon

....

The pride of moon,
The pride of sun,
The pride of earth,
All vanish with an eclipse,
With the clouds blocking the face of moon,
Face of the sun,

....

(234)

An Unknown Author

....

Me an unknown author,
My existence as a writer,
Knows no meaning of existence,
Attempts & persistence,
Killing time of my poor existence,
Dressing the words,
The sentences unknown,
An arrow for the target,
Thou my beloved readers,
Waiting at the door of impatience for feed,
Your feeders my soul's food,

....

(235)

Whether to live or leave

I do not want to leave,
I do not want to live,
The distinct meanings,
Live & leave,
Live & leave,
The fulcrum of life,
Pulls the triggers of my sounding beats,
Every moment an uncertainty,
Looms over the atmosphere,
Questioning the foundation,
Whether to live or leave?
In between the jaws of live & leave,
A suffocating choke,
My confused existence,
All the more complicates..

(236)

Excavating the Great Works

....

The pride of the poet lies in his works,
May not be in lifetime,
But in the aftermath,
The world honors his work,
The World honors his stock,
Whether dead or alive,
The poet writes the epic,
For people of his times,
Contemporary situations of his chimes,
When the earth is dug,
Excavation of the work will come to hug,
The palm leaf writings,
Stored in the museums,
Whoever comes never knows,
But just gives a look at the rusted leaves written in words,
A poet does it for the millions of his wards,
The right direction for a poet to abhor.
The Born feelings in Nature.

....

(237)

The Incredible Gel

From the tummies gel,
Spider weaves the web,
The house swiftly stands,
In the corner of the house,
In between the bushes,
One end of the gel connecting,
Forming a hexagonal arcade,
The fine thread miracle gels,
Built the cobweb in seconds,
None ever seen,
When the spider built the inn,
It is spider home,
A hunting dome,
Insects to crickets in the cobweb,
The spider never goes hunting,
The tiny flies in mirage counting,
Fly into the web's secret threads,
The spider rears the home in comfort,
The gel is spinneret,
An angel that the built the minaret,

(238)

The Ailing Heart

The ailing heart,
Forgetting to beat,
Stopping en-route,
From hell to heaven,
The awesome flight,
The owner's kite,
Finishing it's bytes,
Flying like the kite,
Heavenward,
No one could guess,
How it left the beats,
A happy death,
Blessing in truth,
When the holder does not breathe,
The world posts the wreathe,
Messages flow,
Rest in peace Oh! deserted soul,

Halted emotions appear slow,
All his mundanely possessions,
Remain open,
Only his closed affair with destiny,
Readies him for the last journey.
Once gone,
For ever gone,
The cardinal truth time & again.

....

(239)

The Aftermath

Unless you are gone,
They do not learn,
They just mourn,
Carry your urn,
For immersion,
In the sacred river,
The flowing waters of the river,
Absorbs all whatever,
In its depths of silence,
Hides the soul's existence,
In its depths of darkness,
Hides the soul's awesome existence,

(240)

The World Environment Day

. . . .

Moss green Mountains,
Moss smoky fountains,
Cascading water from the streams,
Pouring like rains from the hilly realms,
The gorge beneath,
Dark green waters in breath,
Moss green smoky rocks,
Unbridled Moss Mountains,
Green house of natural fountains,
Man can't step,
Nature's hidden trap,
Eyes behold,
The beholder knows the hold,
Lovely woods,
Dark & deep hoods,
Insects & centipedes in dome,
Nature truly lives here at home,
The mind can't imagine but capture,
The library of nature,
Has beautiful treasure,
Majestic picture of hilly terrains,

Hilly tribal domains,
Freedom of the animals,
Nature knows it's prettier malls,
Round the clock abundant sun-shine,
Round the clock incessant rains,
The fountain's enigmatic silence,
It's nature the omnipotence,
Known for its benevolence
Sheer presence of green forest in bliss,
Only rare snakes to centipedes,
To wild animals breathe in peace.

....

On the occasion of World Environment Day.

(241)

Save the plank

....

Nature is the best guardian,
The best ever custodian,
Human ministrations,
Causing devastations,
Nature's abundant plantations,
Destroyed by man for his own ministrations,
Men think the universe is their alone,
Forgetting the flora, fauna & other animal,
Massive felling of trees,
Causes havoc of heating the planet,
Innocent plantations,
For selfish human designs,
Divinity please alight,
Give the plants hidden weapons,
To defend their own brethren,
Lest idiotic temperament of man,
Causing devastation,
Incessant felling of trees is no human option,
Plant a tree save the environment,
There is a reason.

....

(242)

The Blind Edge of Life

....

Life is a blind edge,
Even if you live for age,
But the edge,
Blindly attracts,
Play on the edge,
Never know the depth of the fall,
Just immeasurable,
Just unforgiveable,
Death waits at the other edge,
Life here on the stage,
Immaculate thin line divides,
The edge's aging strides,
A blind alibi thou name of life,
The edge controversies age in rife,

....

(243)

The Sleeping Beauty...

....

A midsummer night's dream,
Wakes me up to delirium,
Hearing my noises the dream,
Leaving away from me,
Somnambulistic steps of wandering,
Dash against the wall with falling,
When senses resume,
Realize the mundanely assume,
Hold on to the solid walls,
Fear can't drive me away beyond the walls,
Rock solid faith of the mind,
Clings for safety to be kind,
The crutch misses the hold,
Repudiating me to the sleep's blind fold,
Slumber silently catches up,
Fathomless kingdom of the sleep,
Loves me seeing in its domain,
Embraces the senseless edge again,

....

(244)

The Mist in Atmosphere

The little dinghy,
The handle of the oar,
The white attire,
Reflecting the images,
Of the boat,
Life,
The oar,
The mist of the atmosphere,
The reflections of the green trees,
On the shore,
From one end to other,
Feelings eternally run ashore,

(245)

The Prison of Youth...

. . . .

In the prison of your heart,
You imprisoned me in your youth,
You inhaled air into the affair,
I exhaled the air,
In the inhaling & exhaling affair,
My little heart at times rested inside yours,
My passion was hunting me with you,
Obsession with the little space,
Always sought a place,
The prison doors never opened,
The prisoner remained always locked,
The prison was youth,
That locked my budding youth,

. . . .

(246)

The Imprisoned Lovers...

The prisons locked us in youth,
Ate the finer moments in truth,
Life was a beautiful cage,
Like caged birds we loved the phase,
Love was the only passion,
Time took moments by ransom,
In the prime of youth,
Never imagine what happens in truth,
Locked always in each-other's embrace,
Always lost in the sensuous pace,
Cautious moments,
Moments of frozen sentiments,
Molten lava of the flames,
Burnt up passions to claims,
The prisoners in lock up,
Dreams hatched even in lock up,
Pollens were planted in the wombs,
Budding petals in the tombs,
Blissfully growing in the womb of oblivion,
The primordial connection,

Faithfully lived the moments,
Ecstasy of the prison living the moments,
The prisons eternal locks,
Youthful ecstasy in trunks,
Vision of the love grill,
Gives the occupants lifelong thrill,
The songs of grilled youth,
Heard with emotion of the beautiful truth,

....

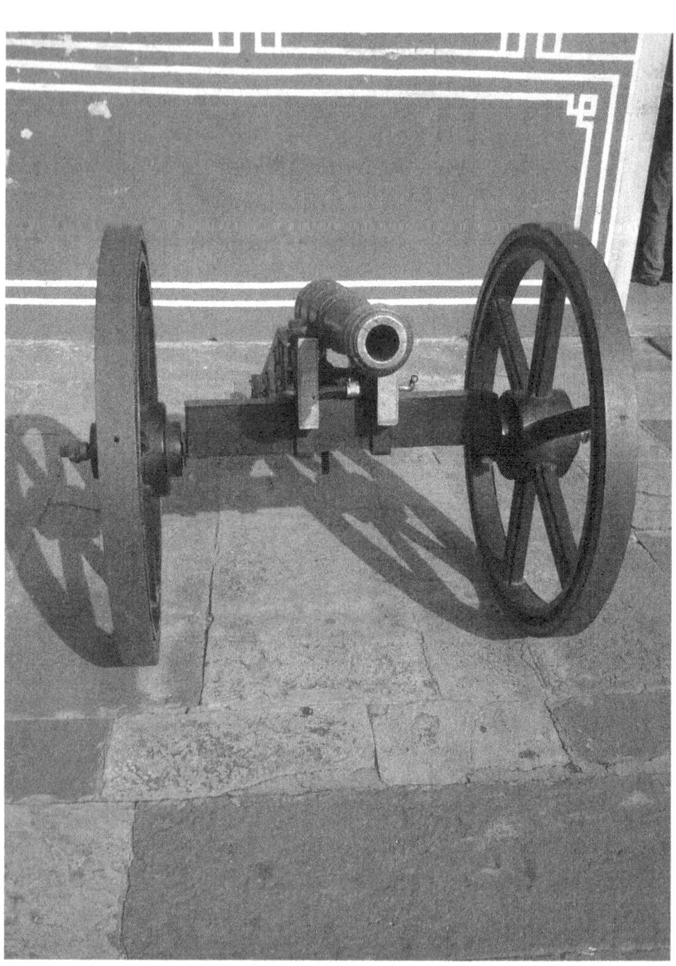

(247)

The Cannons Ire

. . . .

The cannon of mouth fire,
The vengeance packed of ire,
The cannon of eyes fire,
Visionary glances of hatred in ire,
The cannon of verse,
Verse in terse satires,
The cannon of ears,
Listens the dirty words with fear,
The cannon of touch,
Ignites the dormant passionate punch,
The cannon of smell,
Spreads the fragrance ringing the atmospheres' bell,
The cannon of life,
The hard disk burns throughout in rife,
The cannon of laughter,
Eases the situation blowing out the matter,
The cannon of sorrow,
Always grouses like the sparrow,

The cannon of tears,
Wets the cheeks wears,
The cannon of smile,
Wins the million dollar pile,
The cannon of blood,
Connects the families road,
The cannon of death,
Betrays life's tragic faith,

....

(248)

The Nostalgia

Nostalgic expeditions,
Heart sails miles,
In the raft of life,
Sailing the cunning river,
At places deeper in density,
At places transparent sands,
At places camouflaging false sandy graves,
Expeditions have a hearty bickering,
The trekkers pleasure of pride,
Heart does not measure the fathom of happiness,
The engrossed journey of nature,
No boredom,
Every passing phase opens a new image,
A newer invent for the wandering mind,
The wanderlust traveler with his little raft,
Sails fast in the rocky bed of the river,
Risking life at every turn,
The soul in oblivion rafting for fun,
The wonderful nature sails along,
In both ends scenic plantations of nature,
The nostalgia unravels the mysteries,
Life's journey have gimmicks at every bend,
The rhythmic nature playing with the mind.

(249)

The Rain Drops

Dropping in the ocean,
The ocean would absorb,
The drop in the vastness of its being,
You rejoice & relish,
Get drunken in the within-ness.
In the vast stretch of waterbody,
You are a little angel drop,
The ocean solicits the rains,
To wash its surface with distilled waters,
The heavens burst into roaring tears,
The tears fall into the oceans beautiful rear,
The horizon wears the ambers color,
The patches of clouds shining whiteness,
The ocean's vastness is geographic mystery,
Three fourth of the universe is ocean's history,
The little drops of water from heaven,
Fall into the ocean's beautiful oven,
From the little evaporation clouds are born,
Amassed clouds drop droplets of rain,

(250)

The Bitter-most Satires

. . . .

Hunger is a human satire,
Great thoughts battle in fear,
Empty stomachs slavery just tear,
Struggling for a morsel of grain,
Granaries are wasted in the storehouse in vain,
Human Struggle of the empty stomach,
Burns with the empty sack.
Wangering mendicant of day & night,
With empty stomach fight,
Human hunger the real ache,
The pain intolerable with acid bake,
Tons of food grains dumped in vain,
Hunger caused by rain,
The deadline drawn between,
The have's & the have not's,
Left to destiny they just rot,
Begging bowl for little alms,
Compassionate claims,
The donor feels greater demeaning the beggar,

A coin dropped give a million dollar,
Smiling face of the donor,
In poor man's prayer.
The donor's pride remains,
Beggars face appear trodden,
This great division in distribution,
Some roll in opulence while some stifle to breathe,
Is this the sacrament testimony of the living?
Betrayed faith of humans sighs heaving.

....

(251)

Indebtedness

. . . .

Your inspiring compliments,
Make me feel indebted,
Another step on the ladder of thoughts,
To climb one more step,
A poem comes to mind,
In between the steps,
Mind wanders at the recognition,
How come soul's feeling,
Open the gates reeling.
An intoxicating drunken affair with feeling,
Get drunk with the wine of words,
In minced hood.
The child's first cry,
Touching the soul's invisible wires,
The Poetic gravity,
Feel the pulse of the child's needs,
Breast feed the child,
The hungry runs wild,
Food for thought,
The cerebral domain,
Pen the universe to be with season,
Hangover's of the indebtedness,
Nurtured by the Baroness.

. . . .

(252)

The Depth Beyond,

....

When the depth invites,
Death bites..
The world beyond,
Feel shaken of the bond,
Life is bond,
Where & when breaks the bond,
None knows the depth beyond.
The ignorant trust,
Mysterious journey of truth,
The immeasurable depth,
Betrayed halfway faith,
Life feels shattered,
The untold pain battered,

....

(253)

The Composed Looks

. . . .

Composed looks,
Poetic stature,
Filled up emotions,
Thoughtful motions,
Poem for girlfriend,
Written with mannered trend.
The engrossed affair,
She your support & strength for stature,
In the journey of life,
Most enduring,
More of acumen,
Her supportive silence,
Your passionate affair,
Sitting in moonlit care,
The Fingers moving through the hair,
Memories unfold,
Treasures untold,
Embracing into a mold.
A caressing beloved,
By your side.

. . . .

(254)

Conjugal Bliss

Fumes & foams,
Of the conjugal bliss,
Ends in peace,
The pulsating moments,
Aftermath in moments,
Symbolism in paint,
Sighs & hisses of the physical,
Breaking bones moaning hysterical,
A dream dreamt for heaven,
The heavenly happiness with fun,
Electric feelings in high volt,
Even in Himalayas the blissful feast,
Life's goal scored,
Passionate feelings stored,
The drunken moods,
The timber of the soul,
Tuning fumes & rhymes,
To blissful surrender.

(255)

The Imaginary Chariot,

. . . .

The imaginary chariot,
Glowing Wheels,
Journey of life such unabridged,
An empty platform unbridled,
The train of life runs unacknowledged,
Passenger-less on board,
Between the iron rails,
Wheels balancing but life failing,
Does not catch up with the pace,
Vacant unreserved space,
The ultimate ticket collector,
Arrives like a black dog,
Questioning the ticketless travel in vogue,
No plausible answers,
No explanations,
Just a passerby per chance,
In a deserted platform by chance,
Platform after platform,
Like the limbs one after the other in form,
Unabridged,
unbridled,
unacknowledged,
Imagining the sequence of the imaginary chariot...

. . . .

(256)

The Heavenly Drops

....

When rains downpour,
Poets feel being in heavenly tour,
The drops drench them molten,
Words fall like drops from their pen,
The first rains of the summer,
A wild goose chased in hunger,
The thirsty mind to thirsty body,
Vie to cool the mind & body,
The lover's love the showers,
The towers drenched for hours,
The plants drink & bath with the shower,
Love the unseasonal downpour,
Heavens blessings in droplets,
Packed with nectars of the couplets,
The Earth loves being wet,
Life breathed into the earth's heat,
Evaporating vapors,
Flying sky ward in smoky layers,
The grass sprouting green,
The pores of pastures fill in,
The power of shower,
The planet breathes the blissful hour,

....

(257)

A Token of Accolade

Where do I go from here?
When the words,
Blissfully touching me,
Soul for a moment jumping to conclusion,
Soul in silent surge,
Silent expressions in soul's domain,
The ecstatic feelings none can pulse,
The drizzled wet the poet's soul with grace,
Soaked up feelings of solace,
Wisdom playing compassion,
Playing the varied tunes in unison,
Vividly playing with the words,
The poet's mind,
Feelings on piece of paper,
The reader's scissor,
Scissor of pressure,
Bloodless cue in transfer,
The vapors from the hot tea pot,
Flying skyward,
The fragrant smell of the leaves,
The poet's passionate tips,
Just dip deep,
Deep fathoms of the sip.

(258)

The Pangs of Separation

....

The cruel silence kills,
Even if you are gone,
Memories replay,
The fallacy of cruelty,
Too much attachment,
Converts to detachment,
Leaving me on the desert to lament,
Lifelong pain,
Given in vain,
If you knew me well,
How could you be so cruel?
I died every day,
Remembering you everyday,
Hangovers of relation,
Bleeding wounds under the guillotine,
Every moment passes in pain,
Happening in vein,
Never could gauge the relation,
Suffer the pangs of separation.

....

(259)

Love is blind

Love knows no barriers,
Love knows no timing,
Love knows no caste,
No colors,
No caste,
No country,
No religion.
Beyond its depth lies its innocence,
It's true bliss.
It's Platonism.
Love is not only in giving,
Love is a give & take feeling.
A mutual faith of trust,

(260)

Triggers

Just a tickle pulls the triggers,
The triggers not to wait,
The body & mind in unison with the beats,
Sighs released from the heart,
The couples slip into the moment,
Tearing into each-other,
The momentary in gear,
Battles of ransom,
Each trying to win over the other,
Those treasured moments of togetherness,
Hunger opens its doors in happiness,
The affair's silent & speechless fight,
The secrets unravel the moods,
The chocolate bar melts to passionate hoods,
The molten lava glistening to slip,
Droplets on the surface,
Dew sitting on grass.

(261)

The Distance of Love

. . . .

With time the distance widens,
Like the setting sun on the horizon,
Life was leaving its scales,
Annoying words in place,
Everyday fate changed it's cruel garb,
Dreams do not alight in prickly barb,
Without you by side turbulent sleepless nights,
In the ignited flames of passion,
Burnt to ashes in plights,
Life's molten tears flowing abrupt,
Never taking the name to stop,

. . . .

(262)

One Cult One Faith

Love knows no barriers,
Love knows no carriers,
Love knows no caste,
No colors,
No country,
No religion.
Beyond its depth lies it's innocence,
It's trueness,
It's Platonism,
Love is not only in giving,
Love is in belief,
Love is in faith,
That binds two soul's in one cult,
One faith,
A mutual trust,
Infatuation in myth.

(263)

Breathe till Death

Hiding beneath,
From the reality of truth,
Lies the soul's path,
Life's mysteries a chained faith,
From birth till death,
Unreal stages of oath,
From childhood's whining surrealism,
Adolescent color of prism,
Youth's growling mannerism,
In the beloved's arms,
Breathe taking sweated palms,
Life's ways decaying path,
The whining childhood's broken faith,
Landing in the last stages of the breathe,
Man's act a gimmick,
Ignorant paths unknown tricks,
All pretense link in the chain,
Run in vein,
When one link feigns,
Darkness gropes in,
End in vein,
Breathe in vein,
The hiding in vein,

(264)

The Evaporation

....

Love evaporates,
Into the time's blue skies,
Fading colors faded hues,
The smoky clouds come to rescue,
Float the feelings evaporating abode,
Feelings evaporating from mind,
From the soul's pyramid,
Soul sails on surface,
On the swelling tides huge space,
Rippling waves creating illusion,
Feelings swimming in fusion,
Love's unbelievable evaporation,
Humid temper in atmosphere,
Sweats with the passion in gear,
Love wearing colorless attire,
Evaporating in to heaven's vast care,

....

(265)

GOD in New Attire

....

The incarnation,
The soul in migration,
Divinity in transfusion,
Amidst chanting's of divine ordination,
The priests chanting hymn,
Infusing life into the amassing population,
God leaving the scalp of the old reign,
Order changing the Lord incarnate,
The celebration continues throughout the state,
Devotees in frenzied moods,
Surrendering to Lord's new hoods,
May peace flow with the new?
The Age of truth for the universe to renew,
Truth in usage,
Truth in assuage,

With the new cult,
The new incarnate,
Leave the old body of the inn,
Allowing the new to come in,
Tearing the mid-night,
Alight at home right,

....

On the eve of Reincarnation festival of Lord Jagannath the relic Hindu God of Pura. Orissa, India...July,2015

(266)

The Graph of the Moods

....

In the bay of penance,
The tides of remorse,
Washing the beach's moods,
With its tidal waves,
The brooding mind
Languishing with the hangovers,
Irreversible situation,
Depression in formation,
The mind not in agreement,
With the woes of the moment,
The gravity is immeasurable,
Depth insurmountable,
Dreams washed away,
With the receding tides of the bay,
Penance is no resurrection,
Tidal waves,
The feet of the bay washed all days,
Accumulating visitors,
No concern for waves,
Flowing free is tide's passion,
Flowing unchallenged is tide's obsession,

....

(267)

The Soul's Delight..

The rain flies,
Conditioning the atmosphere,
A prelude to rains,
Before they arrive,
Dense clouds fill up the skies,
The earth looks like a dark house,
For a while,
Innumerable moths,
Arrive to dance,
Inviting the rain God,
To earth's huge greenhouse,
Drenching the huge green pastures,
Flora, fauna to flowers,
Relishing the thirsty souls,
Quenching the soul's appetite,
Dancing rain moths,
Clip their wings in the downpour,
Sail away the little frame,
Into the earth's groves,
Rain the heaven's blessings,

Nectar of healings,
Drink & dance festival,
Festival of the soul's delight,
All quenched soul's,
Appeased with the rains,
Heave a sigh of relief,
From the outgoing pain of the summer's heat,
The earth's hard surface opens in grace,
Plants in greenness raise their presence,

. . . .

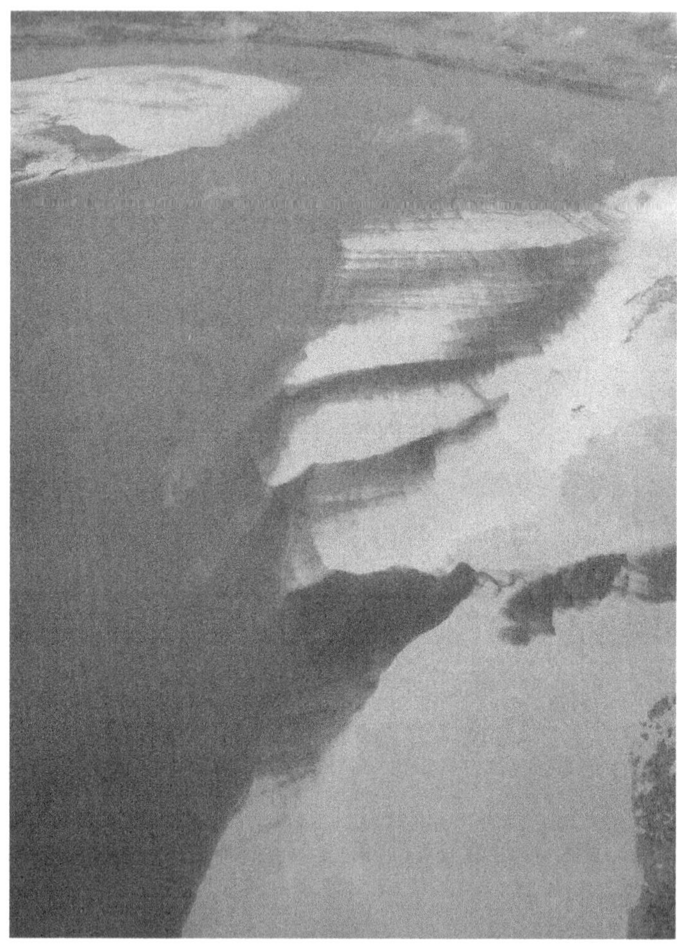

(268)

The Drunken Ambience

....

When dawn opens up its space,
Smiles of solar radiance in opulence,
Walking the tracks with the love,
Home to heaven, bliss in grove,
Radiance of love in presence,
Felt with the dew on the green grass,
Sweats trickle on the faces,
The dawn walking with the traces,
The chirping birds of the dawn,
Sing songs of serenity & fun,
Fabulous feelings smile from within,
Hand in glove men & women,
Walk the ramp of the serene dawn,
Divinity touches the silence of man,

....

(269)

The Stab wounds

When your mentor backstabs,
You have nowhere to go but sob,
Cry aloud & let the tears wash the wounds,
Clean the wounds suffered from backstabs,
Life goes hay ware,
Losing the tenets of existence,
The stab wounds people laugh at,
None comes with the balm,
Even close friends do not forget to harm,
The painful cries fall to deaf ears of destiny,
Steps fall here & there appearing funny,
Enemies to friends all surround to tease,
Pawned life for others to please,
Never confess the mind to any one by mistake,
Hell breaks loose with the confessions at stake,
Some one's tensions become pleasure of others,
Be a mocking bird striking the head for worse,
Everyone behaves like a enemy here,
Silently dislodges you playing the temper,
Keep calm allowing the phase to pass by,
Accept the truths of life bidding good-bye,

(270)

The Orphans of Destiny

....

Not all rivers,
Reach the ocean,
May be the river,
That does not reach the ocean,
Abandoned halfway through by nature,
Drying up resources,
Dying stretches of false sources,
On the sands time vast space,
Does not allow to flow,
The dying existence can't follow,
The intense feelings accumulates,
The accumulation bonding in camouflages,
Woes write grievous wounds,
Wounds not showing up grievous woes,
The river of sorrow dries,
With tears drying up on the surface,
The river of sorrow dies in harness,
Hiding the pile of woes under the debris of sand,
Barren sands of the rivers,
Do not produce,
Future doors close,
Future hope dies,
Dying at the hands of destiny,
A storm blows inside like a mutiny,

....

(271)

Be Gone By Gone..

Yesterday was another day,
No regrets for the day,
Look for future that waits at the bay,
Surprises & gimmicks in store's tray,
Forget the gone,
Forgive the gone,
Learn to hone,
Absorb the self in truth,
Truth in the real breathe,
When truth wails,
Breathe too wails,
Remain with the present,
The past is gone,
Future a granite stone,
Needs cutting & polish,
Future will glow in bliss.
No regrets for the yesterday's happenings,
Remain unchanged & start anew,

(272)

The Little Possessions...

....

A poet has no summer,
No winter,
A poet is all weather,
All season' s,
Not known,
When thoughts,
Command him to write,
Whatsoever,
May be in the harsh heats of summer,
The poet writes the snow clad winter,
A poetic attempt to chill the hearts of the reader,
In the dying heats of the summer,
Springs an eternal choice in atmosphere,
But unless the cuckoo sings,
The pen sits idle,
Scribbling no sense,
The poet's vision the readers,
The Poet waits for the words,
Token of accolades,

His pride,
His little possessions,
His little home,
Poetic passions,
Adores the readers,
The little heart,
To beat,
Beating for the readers,
For exotic words,
An adieu the poet eternally revers,
Little love from the readers,

....

(273)

The Frozen Dreams

....

Snows of the winter's form ice,
Bonding with the winter's chilling freezes,
Roads to trees wear the attires,
The mirror of winter beautifully reflects,
Nature's frozen dreams,
Gravity's rainbows,
Winter's rich characters show up,
The season's depth greets the planet's hope,
The planet's blanket of snows,
Amazes the survivor's with nature's chilling blows,
Old men freeze to death,
With suffocating wind pipes to breathe,
Nature's seasonal character,
The planet teaching behavior,
Renewing the faith of the survivor,
The Survivor seeking blankets for little warmth,

When the season shivers the planet,
The season continues it's woes,
The log of woods provide the warmth,
The season greeting the survivors with renewed faith,
The season has its childhood,
Its adulthood,
Death comes to abdicate the wood,
The season's reign comes to end,
When spring taking the turn & nature's bend,

....

(274)

Hello Dad

. . . .

Happy Father's Day to you Dad.
On this auspicious occasion please bless your lad,
You are the inspiration,
You are the God of all seasons,
Without you we would not have seen,
The light of the world full of fun,
May you live long?
May you walk all along?
Hold our fingers all along,
We will give our shoulders,
We are your true soldiers,
You have taught us the battle of life,
We will fight with your blessings with a swipe,

. . . .

(275)

The Vanishing Castle

....

Dreams are like sand castles,
Dreams resemble childhood orgies,
Whining attitudes,
At times trampled after built,
At times destroyed with a tilt,
Elders do not at times understand,
An iconoclast kicks your castle,
In moments the childhood dreams tussle,
You cry aloud engage yourself building another castle,
Another castle of your dreams,
But alas life's uncertainties,
Broken castles,
A false world of false promises,
No one knows,
When the castle breaks in silence,
You search,
But no remains,

....

(276)

Sailing with the Clouds

Amidst the swimming clouds,
Soul searches bliss,
Soul swims for ashore,
If the clouds could hold for,
Mountain of clouds,
The blue sky's bedecked decors,
A cloud walk just unimaginable,
Pushing through the density paddle,
Oh! cloud do not disperse,
Cover me under your covers,
Soul loves being lost,
Be nature's host,
Depthless feelings,
Captive moods of fathomless,
Pelting the glances,
Pelting the soul for deeper bliss,
Clouds give a feeling oblivion,
Moods of transcendental fusion,
The reader to the visionary,
All awestruck spell bound beyond the boundary,

(277)

The Archives of time

The villa breathes beneath,
The sands sleep with,
The horizon with clouds,
Vision dances proud,
The river bed's wet earth,
Sing a song of peace in hearth,
Vacuum all around,
Green cities with blue skies surround,
The mass of sand stretch,
Countless particles in patch,
The blurred footprints of time,
Lying since birth of time,
Histories buried underneath,
Excavating mind digs the teeth,
In the buried cupboards,
The dug out skeletons,
Dragons to lizards,
Elephants to humans,
Ancient kingdoms,
To flourishing civilizations,
Buried underneath the carpet of time,
Time hides them with the carpet with chime,

(278)

The Nectar of Nature

. . . .

The sand bench,
Nature's lovely trench,
Depth of the blueness,
Reflected on the river's flowing waters,
From one end to the other,
Beautiful decor of Mother Nature,
Even sandy bed of the river,
Holds the reservoir,
The nectar of nature,
Flowing in the river,
The agriculture fields,
To the wild,
Wait for the flow of the nectar,
The rain waters accumulate,
Run seaward for the ultimate,
Desire to flow into the infinity,
Fulfilling the dreams of the eternity.

. . . .

(279)

The Vacuum of life...

....

When my own image stares at me,
Feel pity at my existence,
Even if the mirror beautifully reflects it,
My woes never forgive,
With all mundanely possessions a feeling of vacuum,
Mundanely pleasures do not attract,
Enough of mundanely possessions,
Enough of mundanely attachments,
Utter falseness boasts of pride but does not console,
The ailing soul prefers a hideout,
Even in abundance life's falsities repudiate,
Repudiating my existence at the mercy of time,
Languishing shamelessly in dark corners of the hive,
Shadows are falsified images,
Abandon the mundane world for better spaces,

....

(280)

The Ambush...

An ambush unknown,
Strikes sudden,
From shadows of life,
From camouflage,
From a hideout,
The operation takes start,
The behavior of animal nature,
Like a colorless chameleon,
Change like a scion,
Strategic ordination,
Silently devour the enemy,
When the strike happens,
Simply unpredictable,
The ambush takes place,
To invade the enemy camp,
Destroy the enemy's plans,
Mind is an unpredictable page,
Unpredictable just happens,
Raise the hood for fanatic gains,
Fanatic ambitions reign the mind,
Conquering ambitions rule unkind,
An ambush like a mirage,
Appears & vanishes from nowhere on stage,
Life needs preparations to face,

(281)

The Celebrations,

....

Family bonds renew,
Invoking the new,
The change,
That cometh,
Ritualistic symbols,
Symbols of welcome,
Come the happening,
Musical choirs,
To jubilant dancing,
Unbridled jubilations,
Music of life,
The groom enters home,
With the newly wed bride,
Entering life,
To Celebrate life,
Celebrations of love, fortune & time.
Seek blessings Oh! New Couples.

....

(282)

The Exile..

. . . .

Life is exile,
Birth till death,
Live with inhale,
Leave with exhale,
A grilled jail,
We feel wild,
Inside the grill,
Never knowing,
Our own existence,
That is in exile,
A bane or boon,
None knows,
But history never
Remembers,
After the ordeal,
Belied, betrayed,
After the last inhale,
After the last exhale,
Leave the exile.

. . . .

(283)

The Final Invitation

While leaving for heaven,
I was chanting Amen! Amen!
The hall was full of men & women,
My body was lying stale,
For the family it was a gale,
My face was looking pale,
My soul was readying for the heaven,
Everyone crying sobbing in remorse,
My sorrow none could trace,
Vanishing into the vacuum,
The ether had left leaving the soul to roam,
Steps towards the burial,
The ground was readying for the burial,
The earth's open heart,
Readying to accept,
The pall bearers,
Burn the stale body with fire,
The urns & ash collected for,
Emersion into the sacred river,
With the last rites everything gone,
Death comes in the end for everyone.

(284)

Hopeless feelings

When hopes go,
Hopes die,
Feel killed,
Dreams desert,
Painful pricks,
Bleeding profusely,
Hopes of satire,
Drying with the river,
Work without hope,
without work,
Meaningless existence,
Hopes vanishing,
Leaving no traces,
Misery in faces,
Death bell rings,
On the hopeless existence.

(285)

The Wine of Life...

Life is wine,
As you consume more,
Intoxication consumes to soar.
The unpredictable happens,
Senseless acts,
Committed by life,
Infancy to childhood,
Childhood to adolescence,
Adolescence to youth,
Youth to manhood,
Manhood to old age,
The chain follows one after the other,
Each peg of consumption,
Lives you in confusion,
For ever meaning of life?
Questioning the ageing strife.
Show up fully blown,
The wine never leaves one,

The wine consumes everyone,
When the bottle goes empty,
One leaves empty,
Emptiness to vacuum,
Holding emptiness inside the bottle,
Holding the bottle,
Throttling life,
Drops of wine,
Intoxicating life,

....

(286)

The Stolen Ambience...

Stealing the night's colors,
Night's wilderness,
The flower spraying glamor,
The glamorous night queen,
Her beautiful petals & fragrant scents,
Soothes the mind, heart & soul,
For a metaphysical connect,
The resurrection takes place,
Life's dreams giggle,
The surrounding atmosphere,
Breathing scent with pungent perfumes,
Bliss alighting with night's depth,
oblivion cascading in faith,
The transcendent,
Fragrant riders.
Fills the soul's corridors,
The depth of darkness,
Carves a niche in the queen's prowess,

(287)

Shining Droplets of the Youth

....

Drenched up booties in rains,
Rains dissolve the body with embrace,
The white cloth can't hide the beauty in grace,
Wild mind seeking a hideout,
Afraid of the lonely street,
The beloved can't resist,
How do I?
Oh! Rains can't you wait...

....

(288)

The Bedouin Lifestyles

With the glistening sand particles,
The desert shines,
The sand dunes sleep,
Showing the bare hip,
The Bedouin caravan,
Excavating the myths,
Breaking the desert's silence,
The date palms mute stand,
Watch the desert's golden strand,
The stream of camel's caravan,
Grazes the grass near the oasis,
Drinks the cold waters with peace,
Quenching the thirst of the long journey,
Life in a desert with the Bedouin folk,
Men, women & children all walk,
Open air camps put up to cook,
The Bedouin families write a story book,
Book of stretching vacant space,
Walking the live race,
Eke out a living,

With the bond of family breathing,
The desert's queen camels,
Love the deserts gale,
The deserts silence,
The rider perched on the back of the camels,
From one end to the other travel,
Ringing the neck bells,

. . . .

(289)

The sparkling Melodies..

....

The beauty of the night,
Hides with the love overnight,
Love dreams of beautiful kite,
Flying the wishes to the sky's height,
The beauty of the night,
Winks from the blanket of darkness,
Lovers embracing the night's grace,
The night provides a huge space,
The lovers fearlessly undress,
Unbutton the soul's unquenched desires,
Unbridled passion igniting flames,
The highs & lows of the miracle in bliss,
Bliss of togetherness,
In duress,
Lovers beseech night to be curious,

....

(290)

If Someone could be mine.

If someone could be mine,
Whom I could call mine,
Even if not near,
But far away from mine dear,
But if someone could be mine alone,
Neither sleeps in the sighs,
Nor tears in the eyes,
In dreams we could swim the night throughout
If someone could absorb the woes,
Someone could have been mine,
Someone could have been,
Forgotten promises,
Forgotten memories,
Solitude be there throughout the night,
Some hope survives,
Someone there,
Whom could have called mine.

(291)

The Aroma Merchants...

The street hawkers selling jasmine,
Garland to bedeck the woman's fragrant appeal,
Eking out a living,
Struggle for life time,
Daily sale of pure flowers,
Pawning life at the cost of aroma,
An occupation to pure obsession,
Appeasing the aroma loving women,
Appease the goddesses,
Appease the customer with the adulteress,
Never take the name of ending,
For some the profession,
For many the passion,
From childhood to womanhood,
Struggles a fashion since childhood,
Family profession pursued,

Selling by the street side,
In the small bamboo bucket,
The free vending ticket,
Life knows no seasons for them,
Be it summer, be it rain sale is livelihood for them,
Selling from umbrella's dark shades,
During rains the wet buds,
Customer's prize buds,
Bartering the livelihood.

. . . .

(292)

Oh! Clouds

. . . .

Curtain of clouds,
Hiding my blue face,
The canopy's soulful tears,
Do not hide my beauty,
Oh! Clouds,
Earth my love,
My passion,
A moment's desertion,
Meaningless existence,
The platonic affair,
Do not hide my face,
My beloved weep,
With your raining tears,
Sparks of lightening,
Bullets of thunder blasts,
My beloved would panic,
Oh! clouds remove your curtain,
For beloved's shake,
Do not stand between me & my love.

. . . .

(293)

The Lotus Blooming

The lotus in bloom,
At my neighbor's home,
Looting the dawn's ambience,
Unique pink petals,
Soak the soils of the soul,
With compassion at life,
Learn to walk in rife,
The hidden treasures,
Hiding within the petals,
The stump in mud,
The leaf afloat,
Droplets tilting on leafy surface,
Like glass bulbs rolling without moss,
Evaporating the bulbs into its space,
The petals open up smiling,
The morning goes passionate dolling,
Filling the atmosphere with feeling,
Blissful surrender of the morning,
The lotus goes blooming,
The eyes fixed over the beauty smiling...

(294)

The Golden Memories

....

At times,
Memories leave a painful stretch,
As one ruminates over the past,
The best part regrets,
Ah! My golden era was that.
The worst part regrets,
Silently blinking at the worst part.
Ah! My worst part was that.
Memories be it pleasant or sad,
Always painful.
The grey matter's data bank,
Stores the memories in the archives,
Suddenly a clue of some incident,
Triggers in the library of the archive,
Page after page unfold of the unseen images,
Silent screening on the soul's vast page,
Projecting pictures of pain & pleasure on stage,
Life, love & fortune in the corridors of time,
Memories of the hero in soul flash back,
Glimpses of the heroine in memory's wall catch back,
Brooding over those hangovers gone with the wind,
Languish in the corridors of memory,
Sweeping the pastures of treasury,

The broom of the soul sweeps,
Silent ruminations,
Counting the prices paid for,
Paying the penance,
To the forgotten memories,
Forgotten in time's vast space,
Memories go with life,
Live with life,
Ending in the last breathe.
Memory a written truth.
Memoirs of every man a huge treasure,
For posterity to glance in pleasure...

....

(295)

The Pyramid sleeps in silence...

. . . .

The truncated images of your memory,
The half broken promises torturing,
The skeleton of the promises under the pyramid,
Is nothing but a mummy to be engraved?
The dried flesh has turned blue,
Clutching the bones of the human whose who?

. . . .

(296)

Between the Real & the Surreal...

....

The real world is painful,
The real world is material,
The real world is physical,
Abdicate the real world,
Live in the surreal world,
The surreal world is immaterial,
The surreal world is metaphysical,
Accept the surreal abdicate the real....
The real is mortal,
The surreal is immortal...

....

(297)

The cost of existence...

. . . .

Struggles before humanity,
The struggling colors fighting apartheid,
The struggling professions,
Struggling for the daily bread,
Toiling the day long for little food,
Eke out a living from day one,
Pulling the rickshaw of life day long,
In a world of have's & have not's,
The wealth of the immeasurable gap hunts,
While one relish in opulence,
The other dies failing to find little space,
Question marks rise on the cost of existence,
Whole life hard labor never gave any happiness,
A tent for the family becomes existence,
Shifting from places to places,
To find little solace,
Little space,
Penance for the price of existence,
For the life that never could be the sufferer's choice...

. . . .

(298)

The Butter in wings,

....

Envy the beautiful butterfly,
Flies with butter in wings,
From flower to flower,
Ravishing bruising the pollens,
Stinging the petals soft pads,
Carrying the pollen dusts,
Ignorant carriers of nature,
Pollinating the plant to pregnancy,
What a beautiful pollination,
Unseen acts gifting a beautiful emotion,
When the flower blooms,
Blooms to it's radiance,
Thoughts of opulence,
Crashing the gates,
The bridge of the soul blown away,
Splinters of the pieces lye,
The fruits of love's labor not lost,
Delivered on time,
The awesome theories of evolution,
A genius is born,

....

(299)

Truth alone Triumphs...

Truth is soul,
Soul is truth,
Truth is religion,
Truth is power,
Truth is love,
Truth is life,
Truth is time,
Truth is source,
Truth is opulence,
Truth is the best companion,
Live with truth,
Love the truth,
Leave with truth,
Truth is non-violence,
Sans truth,
No meaning in life,
Truth is peace,
Exist in Peace.

(300)

Scared of the sting...

A big scorpion's dead scalp,
Trampled under some unknown wheel,
While crossing the road from one side to the other,
Crushed to death,
Lying abandoned leaving breath,
My passerby mind could not resist,
Captured the scalp for a post,
The innocent pays a price,
Prying into the urban spice,
Insects to scorpions to the wild animals,
All run away to hibernation for peace,
Human slavery cordons them in sanctuary,
The planet has mysteries hidden inside,
Animal's destiny never known,
A pure choice of life,
Procreation of their brethren,

Live as long as life permits,
Whether tenure is over or not,
Longevity at times a cancelled permit,
A scorpion, a snake, a centipede to an ant,
Everyone has a gifted weapon of sting,
They live with the moment in their being,
In the domain of their little wisdom,
Without knowing ever what life is,
Scaring one of the sting.

. . . .

(301)

The Meteors

....

The aliens really came,
Like meteors they came,
Created a wonder for me,
They came like a gale,
Storming into the platform of my dell,
Thoughts just reveled,
My poetic mind just regaled,
Flown to the heavens,
Rocking on the cradle,
My poetic words in the swivel,
Swiveling lines of poems on scribble,
Scribbling words of bliss on the dell,
Feeling as if aliens just flew down my corridors,
The corridors of my grey matters,
The pastures signaling me the caricatures,
Signaling my fingers,
Little finger to ring to middle to the index and the thumb,
Last but not the least,
Infinite feelings,

Blasting the furnace in fire,
The passion in full ire,
Flowing sequence of a symmetry,
Abysmal faith bonding in the geometry,
The asylum of my soul feeling the beauty,
Wondering if aliens really alighted to do their duty.
Doing their duty.

....

(302)

The Trajectory of time..

Time gives,
Time snatches,
Life is a beggar at time's doors,
Time nurtures life,
Watering the plant of life,
Flowering the plant,
Giving fruits to the plant,
The plant breathes time,
From child to man singing the beautiful rhyme,
Rhyming the music of age,
From twinkle twinkle little star,
To rose,
From dreamland to reality of old age,
Reminding humanity the beautiful adage,
The adage of time,
The entry & departures gates of time,
Life is a beautiful puppet's ring,
The puppets dance to the command of the string,
Swinging into the drama of life,
Playing the roles directed in hype,
The audience watching mute,
Clapping to the excellent acts put,

Onstage performance beautiful mimicry,
Laughter at times to at times cries,
The intentions never known,
Just a silent wink at the past frowns,
Real acts in the hindsight,
Puzzles unsolved left & right,
Timers fixed for every action,
Every action has equal & opposite reaction,
The irony of life remains a mystery,
Beautifully preserved in the museum of history,
The ultimate truth prevails,
The truth alone hails,
Time knows the art of giving,
The art of living.

....

(303)

The Mahout knows.

....

The mahout
Alone knows,
How to handle,
The elephant,
The elephant,
That life is..

....

(304)

Sneaking through the windows.

. . . .

Sneaking through the windows,
We dressed our emotional woes,
The trespass in camouflage,
The flames of the mind in real rage,
Just burn the burning disks,
Least caring the risks,
The youth in frisk,
In moments husk,
Tight hugs,
Bitten by the love bugs,
The reddened lips,
Marks on the unknown cliffs,
Visibly love beaten,
Nothing to eat only love was eaten,
Still the fears of uncertain,
The tears flowed for certain,
Washing the wounds of romance,

Stinging for hours feeling trance,
With blank cups of tea,
Sipping the words like a bee,
Smoothening the soul,
Even if the age was playing role,
Committed acts of ambush,
Ignorant manners filled the bliss.
Sneaking through the windows,
Dressing the woes.

....

(305)

In the Beloved's hold...

In precious hold of the sweet sixteen,
Passion writes a hurricane.
Until the tempest blew,
Lifted the veil of the dormant volcano,
The molten lava spilling hot,
Ulysses to feel contented...
As we crossed a path never before...

(306)

The Relics of my Ancestors

Relics of ancestral place,
Ruptured memories,
On the walls of history,
Moss grown over time,
Turning thick black lime,
Passion of time,
Longer the gaps,
Lesser the memories clasp,
The lengths of time's corridors,
Changed fast leaving no doors,
As you dig the graves of the pyramid,
You only find mummies in placid,
No one telling the story of time,
Excepting their burnt out frames in rhyme,
Time & tide wait for none,
In the act of receding both gone,
Man is only a mute witness,
Searching the origin baffles his cronies,

(307)

The Craftsman

Whole of life.
Carving myself,
Hammering my odds,
Hammering my evens,
Searching the self for my images,
When I look passionately at me,
My self feels the surprises,
From the carvings,
The images of varied hues,
At times feel dejected,
At times feel ecstatic,
Collecting ounces of happy feelings,
Realizing the Craftsman in me,
Of my mind & soul.

(308)

The Voice of the Seven Chords...

....

The seven chords,
The seven beats,
The classical rhythms,
The voice sings the true reeds,
The trio sung in unison,
Create ecstasy in fusion,
An ambience of intense passion,
Peace scribbling solace,
In soul's secret chambers,
Peace singing the chords of ambers,
A metaphysical hypnosis,
A mystical journey into synopsis,
Transforming the rhyming seven,
Into intense bliss,
The clouds rhyming ignorance in bliss.

....

(309)

The Flames of Passion

An insect's passion for flames,
Fanatic games,
Even if the wings get burnt,
The tiny insect boils in flames,
In wild love for the flames,
Does not deter,
The little insect,
Live in the flames,
Leaves with the flames,
Love the flames,
Die for the flames,
Oath of love,
Even in death,
Platonic breathe,
Cardinal truth,
The creator's choice,
The insect versus,
The flames,
Insect's life in ransom,
With the Flames,
The love between the two,
An eternal bonding.
In life or death,

(310)

The Logistics of Longevity

....

Conditioned longevity,
Dictates of the society,
Fall in values of rationality,
Irrational happenings,
Disturb the innings,
The reduced innings,
Twenty over game,
Overnight name & fame,
Human ambitions touch a new name,
Secret inhibitions,
Older version,
Takes a shift in dimension,
Music & dance becomes modern passion,
Every one dances to the tunes of fashion,
Every girl changes her looks,
With fair & lovely bleaching the face,
From black to white a mad race,

No dress codes,
The brute's un-code,
No one feels safe,
Fear of scathe,
Fear of the demons roaming traps,
Pack up & move out of the traps,
Conditions of longevity,
Outlives the logistics,

....

(311)

The Bubbles of life

....

Inside a water bubble,
A dancing couple,
Beyond the bubble,
Life plays dribble
Life a beautiful air bubble,
When the bubble,
Just dribble,
Feelings hail,
The heart feels the gale,
As if life would sail,
Like a grasshopper in trail,
The bubble a miracle,
With bubble life climbs pinnacle,
Without it a sad debacle,

....

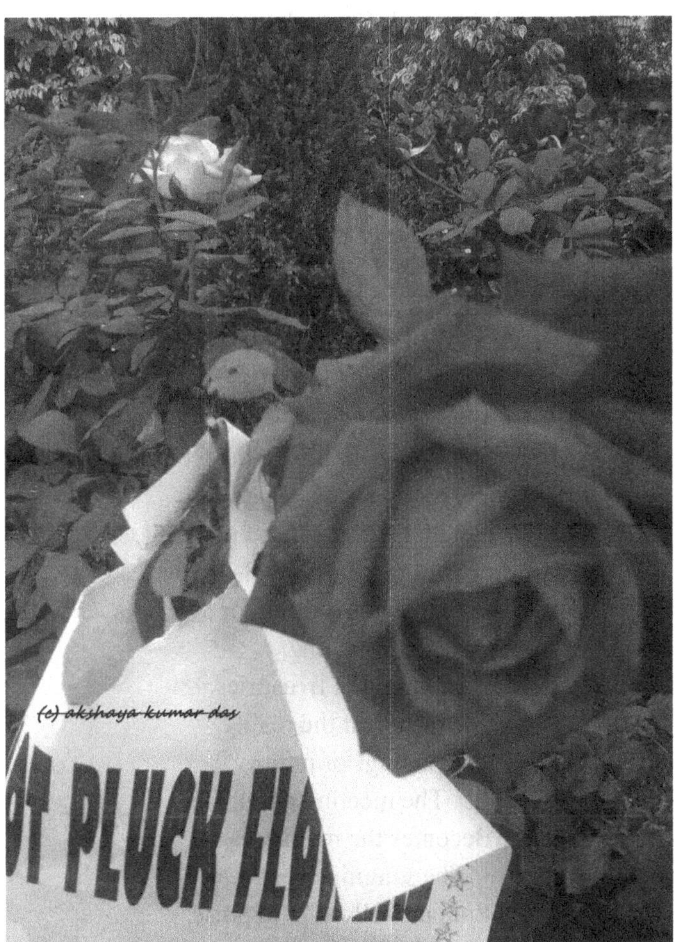
(c) akshaya kumar das
PLUCK

(312)

The Red Rose...

Sanguine blood red,
Petals nature bred,
Wrapped up folders of the petal,
One flower holding the total,
Aroma sprayed in the atmosphere,
The garden feeling the treasure.
Treasure of love in the x-zone,
Lover's take a glimpse,
Embrace in locks,
Locking the lovers,
In golden silence to breath the feelings,
Plays of ecstasy enacted,
Written on the red petals bracketed,
Names engraving symbols of love,
The twin souls uniting for love,
Touching,
Hunting the treasuries,
Smiling at the reality,
Feelings of infinity,
The meeting point,
Becomes the melting point,
The sanguine red rose,
Romantically sigh in poise,
Molten soft ornamental words,
Sung by the soul's woods,
Moods catch up the moment,
The beloved's massage a beautiful foment,

Pricks like the thorns of rose stem,
Bleeds with passion in each claim,
The stakes of the groping eyes,
Playing hide & seek fearing the hunting assuage,
Red Rose is lover's paradise,
Red Rose redness symbolic lips in guise,
The petals soft touch,
Tells the lovers to feel the love's aromatic punch.
Seeking moments in seclusion,
The red rose dreams lover's in fusion,
The pollens of the red rose,
Seek pollination hunting the bees,
The humming bees stealthily make an entry,
Stealing the pollens fly to another point,
The do not pluck symbols never deter,
The lover's meeting every second, minute & hour,
Anxieties of the lovelorn couplet for the ensuing tour.
Pulse of the beloved's battling forever.

....

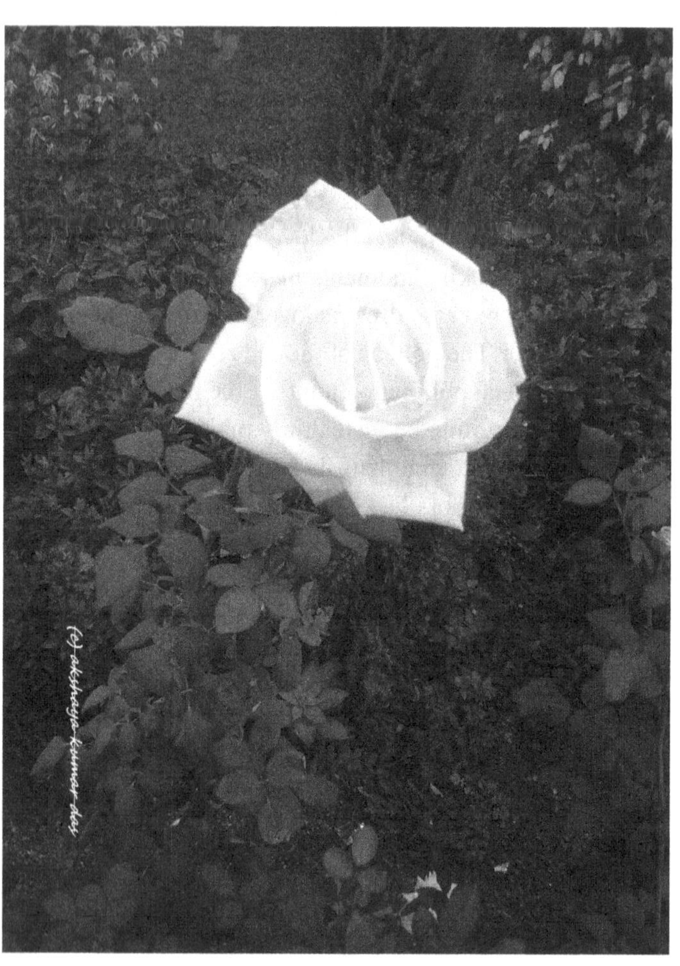
(c)-akshaya-kumar-das

(313)

A White Rose..

....

Peace in symbolism,
The beautiful petals,
Layers over layers,
Nature's boutique,
Beauty in radiance,
Queen in trance,
The sinner washes his guilt,
The radiance purifying the soul's quest,
The pollens hiding in camouflage,
Inside the budding boundaries,
Petals woven in beautiful bondage,
The radiance of opulence,
Spreads aroma of peace in abundance,
Lover's proud possessions,
The hearts held in ransom,
A rose bud patches up the differences,
Between warring minds to nations,
The fragrance kills the sensuous senses,

Aroma ceasing the nasal trenches,
Thumping accolades & appreciations,
Flows in to fill the golden ambience,
Life is not a bed of roses,
Thoughts for a while pleases,
Life's beautiful dreams are like roses,
Sensuous, sizzling & amorous teases.

....

(314)

The Pains of Life

The old flame hunts like a ghost,
The couples feel breach of trust,
Breach of trust throughout,
The stroke inside the heart,
Ruptures the soul bleeding out,
Life feels shattered too,
Broken reeds of love in fight,
Stifling chokes chasing tight,
For the shake of love a price,
Penance in languish,
Pay the price in silence,
Burn into ashes,
Till life breathes,
Tragic trajectory of love,
Forget me not forgive me love,
Love is a sacred truce,
Live & let live in the beautiful sacrifice.

(315)

The Blank Mind

....

Nothing mind cooks,
Nothing mind hooks,
Thought betrays even reading books,
No stuff for the morning,
Even one cigarette after the other burning,
The mind feels sad in the morning,
Cursing the situation never turning,
A poem for the day must take birth running,
If thoughts do not conceive,
The blank mind fails to receive,
Only vacuum surroundings deceive,
Feel cheated by the situation,
Such unbearable when you go barren,
A barren mind does not cultivate,
Impotence gives nothing to vomit,
When the impotent mind cultivates a barren field,
Not a morsel produced for the community to be fed,
Everyone in anxiety waiting for the morsel of food,
In vein nothing produced when mind fails to cook,
In betrayed moods of the mind the
poet does not give a look.
Nothing mind cooks, nothing mind hooks.

....

(316)

Obituary

....

Friends assembled.
With flowers in offering they prayed,
May the soul rest in peace?
The sad demise,
Family's loss,
Tribute to the family's head,
Paying wreathe in memory,
Family to relatives signing an obituary,
A lamp in memoriam,
The lost soul in photo frame,
The cruel line of faith,
Between life & death,
Broken promises,
Of life in lease,
Lease with death,
Death is the ultimate truth,
When death summons,
Life just succumbs,
The soul of the gone,
In the form of vacuum clone,

Invisible to the naked eye,
Graces the occasion with a moving eye,
The crowd that swelled,
Searching the crowd,
Who remembered?
Who missed...?
The obituary,
In honor of the lost soul's memory...

....

(317)

The poem ending with the "N"

....

Reading a fiction,
Engrossed passion,
Roaring wheels of the running train,
Lying on the berth with attention,
Eyes in concentration,
Line by line,
Story of the fiction,
The train the orphan,
Running with soul's to a destination,
The fiction's pages remain,
With a mark on the page of the brain,
The engrossed affair of the fiction,
Teaches man depth of concentration,
In one breathe read the line,
Before the train,
Arrives at the destination,
The breathe accelerates to completion,
The horror book to one night stands is an ancient passion,
Hercules the poi rot to harlots in the garden,
Line by line mugged up to the reader's brain,
The weary reader in between arrives at the slumber's den,
Dreaming of the story's pages happening in chain,
Hiding the face under the pages of the
book in the running train,

The roaring wheels even silence to the snoring human,
The onlooker's to fellow passengers look at the man,
A horror book's cover pages showing the
cleavages of the book in vain,
The back page boldly publishing the
horror to sizzlers hidden,
Reading a fiction,
Become a travelers best passion,
To fiddle with time of travelling a far off destination.
Reading a fiction,
Once again reminds of the beautiful passion,
Season's best obsession,
Digging the earth's aromatic obsession.
Rotating around the axis of the traveler's destination
Ending the poem with a Nano "n"
Alighting from the orphan train...

....

(318)

Buddha...

....

To the woman who came to him with her dead child,
If you can bring a morsel of mustard seed,
From a house where no death happened,
Assure to wake up the child from death bed...
Hope of a morsel of the seed to the nearby hood,
After many days of tiresome journey
returns empty handed,
The Woman.

....

(319)

The Droplets to satiate.

Droplets to satiate,
The thirsty earth's plate,
Drizzling droplets,
Over the hamlets,
Conditioned atmosphere,
Cheers for the poor,
The nature's air-conditioner,
Chills the atmosphere,
Season's best gift of nature,
Couples fill the wild temper,
Rolling on the hamlet's floor,
The couples weave dreams,
Nature gives pleasure in prisms,
Colors of rainbows shines,
On the heaven's blueness,
The seven hues,
Truly seduces,
Each soul feels ecstasy,
Frenzied moods in fantasy,
Fantasizing the future,
Dream nature,

Conceiving ovens,
Fortifying frozen cells,
Fertilized seeds to eggs,
Sprouting to the drizzling lashes,
Tearing the soils hard surface,
The season's germination,
Granary's waiting in hibernation,
The year's cultivation,
For the earth's population,
June to August,
The green house of trust,
Love's labor never lost,
Wait for the drizzling droplets,
To satiate the thirsty earth's plates,

....

(320)

When Heart is torn

....

When the heart is torn,
The soul loves to mourn,
The loss of emotion,
The loss of the poetic lines raises a commotion,
The nerves stand in erection,
Searching the lines of passion,
Lost in the malfunction,
An obituary of words written,
Poet's cries are best consolation,
The tears are words from the heaven,
Nurture an irony in the soul's domain,
The soul traverses into the forgotten den,
Forgiving the plight of the pain,
The love of the poetic feelings lost in vein,
The famous saying comes saying to err is human,
In the mortal world what so ever you
loss does not comeback again.
Even though hopes confide in the theory of reborn.
When the heart is torn,
The soul in abnegation,
Just burn with frustration.

....

(321)

Exist

I exist or not,
In between the puzzle I exist,
To exist or not.
In subconscious I exist,
Only in the present I exist,
In the night my senses cease to exist,
In the day my senses give me a feel of the exist,
But I ponder do I really exist.
The mystery of exist,
Shrouds the exist,
Evades the exist,
Loves the exist,
Hate the exist,
Succumbs to the exist,
At times in the word I exist,
Only in between the passing breathe I exist,
The philosophy of exist,
I continue to exist,
Without knowing the end to exist,
My helplessness to trace out the beginning exists.
I wonder if I at all I exist,
The "I" truly exist.
The puzzle of the human ego in which I exist.

(322)

The Slum Dweller

....

The slum dweller is a fake millionaire,
Lives a life truly like a billionaire,
The shanty slum around the railway tracks,
Even the quake can't crack,
The roaring noise of rail music,
Everyday soaring sounds of rustic,
The slum dweller has a life of his own,
Enjoys life to the lees without remaining in the own,
The meaning of life is but to live on one's own...

....

(323)

The Humble Gardener

. . . .

The humble gardener,
Guarding like a mother,
Feeding the plants with milk of love,
Prunes the plants with trove,
The plant feels motherly love,
The smiles of the blooming flowers,
Count the gardener's toil & tears,
Nurturing the plant with his iron spades,
Rearing them with velvet shades,
The greenery of the lawn shaped with blades,
Attracts the butterflies to sweet sixteen to fold,
Plant a sapling for the hope of a green future,
Shaping the environment to beautiful treasure,
The gardener breathes life into the garden,
The garden pays tributes to the treasurer of the garden,
Jasmine to amaranth to rose beautify the emotion,
The neighbor's envy owner's pride feeling the possession...
The Esoteric mindset in a mundanely universe,
Since time immemorial a human passion of golden verse,
The gardener weeding the garden,
Softening the soils from being harden,
An act of no less charity in passion,
Soulful tributes to the humble human,
The Humble Gardener.

. . . .

(324)

The Myth of Life

....

Every morning life comes recycling,
Paddling the dawn alighting,
The day to noon to evening beautiful race of tri-cycling,
Moon walking the evening smiling,
Since time immemorial the eternal happening,
The dawn's cool hypnosis such pleasing,
The dawn walks the day till the dusk dreaming,
Life's gears accelerate speeding,
Every living creature engrossed with life flying,
Flying like a colored kite with the thin threads tussling,
Tussling to detach the kite flying,
Brushing against the sharp thread edge of the glue,
The hue of the kite feeling up the gaps of colored hue,
Snapping the ties the kite flies to unknown destination,
To the aliens land of angels and fairy queen,
Renewing the same faith same trust,
The ignorant manners of nature a great myth,

....

(325)

In your Arms

. . . .

In your arms,
Enjoy the charms,
In your kiss,
Enjoy the feelings,
The heart relish,
Enjoy the embrace,
Leave my remains,
Enjoy your hisses,
The heart sighs,
For more of your kisses,
Vying for more,
More of the hidden treasure,
Give me more,
Just surrender,
Youth is short,
Just flies out,
Twinkle of an eye,
Youth flies bye,
Youth to adulthood,

In affairs of life get engrossed,
Life is like a kite,
Glued thin threads to enjoy,
Enjoy the kite fly,
Enjoy the life fly,
Time & love wait for none,
Thoughts in blinks moments gone,
In your arms,
Enjoyed the charms,
In your kisses,
Enjoyed the feelings,

....

(326)

The Poetic Chariot...

....

Driving a nice poetic chariot,
The caravan pulls the lot,
Breathing poetry in silence the poet,
An ominous task to be handled with patience,
Omissions & commitments to be handled with finish,
A poet remains hidden in words,
Failing to wrap around,
Even a small word
Hides nudity,
The poet is nude in poetic frigidity,
A poet can't script when words suffer rigidity,

....

(327)

The Betrayal,

....

Reflections visible on portraits,
Uncanny beards,
Unbroken silence,
Time teases,
At the poor existence,
Piling woes,
Even in death,
Never such remorse,
The abrupt end,
No straw to defend,
Sink into the abysmal,
Depth of the ocean of woe,
Fathomless depths,
Fathomless darkness,
Pale faces,
Stale smiles,
Pensive looks,
Psychic shocks,
Paralyzing the soul's nerves,
Tortuous moments,
Tortuous seconds,
Pulse slowing breathes,
Life taking a toll with wreathes.

....

(328)

The Volcanic Ire

The Dormant Vesuvius,
Flowing in rebellion,
The ire of earth's reddened tongues,
Flowing molten flames & the ever flowing lava,
When the eruption happens,
With a dormant soul,
Breaches all faith,
Breaks all barriers of trust,
Burns every particles whatsoever comes,
The river of flames flooding fire,
Burning boiling the innocent,
Under its fierce wraths,
Cursed for life never to be born,
Hidden in the naked truths,
No savior extends a hand,
When the savior himself lost his hands,
When the whistle of the Vesuvius is heard,
The horizon trembles in fears dreaded,
Silent meanings silent tears playing the music of moan,
Tears flowing to appease the soul's fears,
When the unwanted happens,
Hopes just vanish with touches & sighs,
Crying Alas! Alas!

(329)

The Faith of time

Time is the testimony,
Time is truth,
Once gone never returns,
The mirror of future reflects rainbows,
In the twinkle of an eye,
Darkness reigns,
Light opens its own space,
Particles playing in the shadow,
A long line in fusion,
From one end of the darkness to the other,
Every soul ruminates in silent prayer,
The mysterious path of life,
To feel the specialty,
The long row of fusion reigning silence,
No one will open your eyes,
You have to open yourselves,
Even after a tiresome journey,
Light finds its own ways,
It's understandings,
With the standing situation,

Whatever may appear to be truth?
Truth is truth,
None can hide truth,
Even in the hideout truth opens up its pages,
The blind understanding fails,
One fails to perceive truth,
Blind feelings dominate the mind,
No one defines what truth is,
What truth is?
Truth is absolute.
Soul's enlightenment.

. . . .

(330)

From the Wit's End...

....

Gloom drags the self to depth of the matter,
An atmosphere of monk's silence remains in the crater,
Certain truths better shelved inside the pit,
Unwanted disclosure bares open secret,
The wit at its best balancing the whole act of negativity,
Worsening the conditioned heart to suffocating resilience,
The heart's innocence hides in the grove of silence,
The river of repentance flows in remorseful waves,
The wave lengths touch the sands of the beach,
Kissing the beach's surface with
bubbles receding in the hitch,
The bubbles of penance receding back leaving no sketch,
Mingling into the depth of serenity
hiding beneath the pitch,
Truths of life are rarely told in open,
The character of truth cannot hide but beacons,
In the depth of the gloom hides the secret of life,
Without confession the meaning of life remains in strife.

....

(331)

Oh! Mom Where are you gone

. . . .

Oh! Mom where are you gone?
Just sing me a lullaby,
Show me the crescent moon,
Rhyming a line,
Lull me to sleep,
In your laps lies my heaven,
Oh! Mom where are you gone?
Show me the cloud in your songs,
Show me the blue skies in your whispers,
Lulling me to silence from my whining tempers,
Your songs like chocolates,
Swallowed by my innocence,
In seconds the self loves solitude,
You had a home to look after,
Lest how could you manage my torture,
In my kinder garden playful whining moods,
Knew every nerve of mine,

Cartoons kinder garden songs sung then,
Spending restless nights for me to grow,
Today in the yard of life when I seek you,
A shadow of your image moves around me,
Pouring the blessings even in absence,
Which is a feeling of your magnanimity?
Oh! Mom where are you gone.?
My existence is your true clone.

....

(332)

Death lives in disguise

. . . .

Death lives in the disguise,
Every moment life dies.
Strange ways & meanings of life,
Suspense & shadows creating illusions in rife,
Mirages appearing & vanishing in the twinkle of eyes,
Ruminating over the confusions life,
Mysteries chasing without any noise,
The heart dances in disguise.
Death eternally lives in the guise of life,
Wearing a blanket of falsity in the name of life.

. . . .

(333)

The Longing is Lifelong...

The longing is lifelong,
Memories of the mother,
However aged the child may be,
A child remains a child always for the mother.
Platonic placental connections of infinity,
Soul alone knows the feelings of eternity,
If time could clock back,
The moving hands of time take me back,
To my mother's lap of tender memory,
To refresh the placental resumes in story,
Screening each sequence of the history,
Page by page pearls of the moment's glory,
When the longing is life long,
Why not mom makes a comeback,
To complete the assignments,
Home works for the fake world,

Take me in your laps,
Flying me into the surreal world of yours,
In your pats & embrace lives soul,
I love to be there forever,
In your arms clutching to your shoulders,
Sleep in peace dreaming peace,
Dreaming bliss,
Stay in the the mundane universe,
Eternally shelter in the oblivious.

. . . .

(334)

Uncertain Dreams,

....

Wings of the bird clipped,
The bird even with the clipped wings,
Wish to fly,
The inherent character for the bird is flight,
With the wings clipped she losses her might,
Humming in silence she is in deeper fright,
Whether the child she carries,
Will deliver safely on the trees,
Waiting in the labor pains,
The empty basket dropped in vein,
If god will alight from the heaven,
Awesome may happen.

....

(335)

The Tiny Seed

. . . .

The Tiny Seed,
Never knowing that it could breed,
Even if dumped under the soil,
Fights out,
To sprout
As a little sapling,
The sapling's appealing tiny leaves,
Infuse life into the mystic nature's heaves,
Even from darkness the thin ray of light,
Thin ray of life starts to culminate
The tiny sapling growing into a huge tree one day,
The huge earth in which the miniature exist,
The supernatural powers in true bliss,
The tree never eats its own fruits,
Donates everything to the earth,
To the aliens,
To the humans,
To the earth,

One grows them while another eats,
Great Heart of accomplishment,
The logo of going green message for the humans,
Do not disturb the echo,
Do not destroy the environment,
Plant a sapling,
Plant a tree,
For posterity to breathe peace,
An act of noble nature,
An act of noble gesture...

....

(336)

Tributes to a True Hero...

The great man leaves for heaven,
Mission missile ignited minds man,
Leaves after completing his mission,
A noble man of pious attitudes,
His laurels surpassed the rocketing latitudes,
Unbelievable that he is no more,
The cardinal truths of life leave us in tears,
Man of the planet that he was,
A true genius of many laurels,
His Endless credentials,
Compassionate & cool with a young mind,
Father,
Friend,
Philosopher,
That he was,
Scientist to writer to presidential palace,
Made his ways from grass roots,
Involving his lone self always in the ignited minds,
From defense research to scholarly passions,
A true gifted son of the soil with his
down to earth manners,
The APJ always a cheerful personality with a vision,
APJ an astute person of Joy needs no description,
Morning shows the day,
Sowing the seeds of glorification of the unknown,

Eleventh President of the Republic of India
A person of brilliant vision,
Beating with the common man's
pulse, dreams & aspirations,
A colossal irreparable loss to India & the world vision,
In the last few seconds of life a duty
bound citizen of the Nation,
Even destiny could not detract you
from your dedicated mission,
Believed in the faith of karma (duty)
work is worship passion,
A huge gap for the country with your
demise so sad & sudden,
Left without giving any pain to the nation,
Silently shifting to heavenly domain
completing your mission.
The country will always remember,
Your great contribution,
to
the
NATION.

....

(337)

The Mild Stroke of Yesterday

. . . .

Even the mild tremor could not,
Stop you to desist,
From your passion,
The tremor shakes us,
But poetry lives long,
Lives beyond the Richter scales,
For the sake of passion,
Damn you the stroke of the tremor,
You can't shake the poet's pleasure,
The poet can't breathe in peace,
The poet can't betray readers,
In the Reader's soul the poet thrives,
The poem like blood flows from the pen of the soul,
Oh! Poet of great thoughts you give a real feel,

. . . .

(338)

Me & my Lord

For you my lord,
Me & my god,
Blessing pours from god,
When the duo stand dude,
The bond showing the proud dad,
The bond showing the proud lad,
The true lad of the dad,
The lad bring fame for the dad,
The name of the dad
Be written on the golden pad,
The lad waits for the dad's nod,
Every step walked,
The dad held the fingers of the lad,
Showing him the world,
Be happy my lad,
Be happy Oh! Dad...

(339)

Childhood memories

. . . .

Someone tears the pages,
Books I left on the pavements,
To call on nature,
Returning from school,
En-route home,
Next day teacher,
Opens the pages,
Slaps me hard,
What is this?
How can you tear the pages?
It was a new book,
I cried insolent,
Pleading my innocence,
Could never know when the pages were torn,
The teacher understood my pleadings,
How can I tear my own books?
Teacher smelled rat,
Must be,
Must be someone from the class,
Asks me to fetch,
Palm full of rice with turmeric powder mix,
Run home with my friend in one breathe.

Fetch the palm full of rice with the turmeric mix,
The teacher played a trick,
Chanted some chanting silently,
Hissing into the rice,
Asked everyone in the class to eat
A grain of rice,
Let us see who the culprit is,
The culprit will vomit on spot,
Every one swallowed jolly hot,
Except my cousin the culprit,
Fearing to swallow it,
That was childhood,
The whining cunning naughty childish gimmicks,
Used to rule our lives,

....

(340)

Golden memories...

....

Wearing a moustache,
Imitating Daddy,
Daddy's long shirt,
Looking like a baboon,
Just walked into the neighbor home,
Imitating the tone of my dad,
My neighbor turns up to see the surprise,
It is you the naughty lad,
I will tell your dad.
Oh! Neighbor please do not tell my dad,
Hold your ears make ten sittings,
Said the Neighbor,
Promising not to imitate,
Escaping cunningly from the situation,
By my own mimicries of imitating the dad...
That was childhood,
Memories hunt me to brood,
Travelling down memory lane,
Remembering the childhood den.

....

(341)

Be my bride....

Ask my sister,
Let us play,
A game of marriage,
You be my bride,
Call other children to be partners,
Of the game,
Wear a garland of green leaves,
Sit on a wooden plate,
Put paste of soil mimicking sandalwood,
Tie a towel on the head,
Be the groom,
From one end of the little yard,
The groom's arcade leaves,
To the other end to reach the waiting bride,
Someone whistling,
Someone singing,
Someone playing music from his toy bigul,
The royal arcade proceeds,
The marriage takes place,
One playing the role of priest,
Palms tied into a knot,
The marriage is over,

A grand feast with jackfruit leaves,
Distributing dust & leaves of variety as food,
Food for the grand gala celebrations,
Suddenly mother starts yelling,
Ye come home the food is ready,
Leaving the venue all run,
Forgetting the little charming moment...
That was childhood,
My longings of the heart still brood...
Oh! Childhood why not make a comeback,
To share the treasures the gunny sacks...
Jumping from one to the other back to back...

. . . .

(342)

Oh! My beloved childhood

Never knew rowing ever,
But like a brave soldier,
Held the oar,
To ferry across the river,
Scary people on the boat,
Shouting at the me seeing childish gut,
Pleaded my acumen,
Ferrying was my regimen,
Like an astute ferryman,
As in the middle of the river,
The boat swirls into the water,
My little wisdom was nowhere,
Jumped into the river,
Leaving the boat in middle of the river,
Swam the distance in twinkle of an eye,
Escaping the scolds & slaps saying bye...
That was childhood,
In later age my memories brood,
Once again why not clock back of my childhood...
To sail in the dream hood,

(343)

The Immortal Lover

....

That night she had fever,
She asked me to measure,
Neither was I a doctor,
Nor I had a thermometer,
When I tried to feel the temperature,
I was pulled towards the treasure,
My irresponsible mind went for the venture,
Innocently applying soothing pressure,
The treasure hunt continued into pleasure,
Pleasure of the infinite treasure,
Soon came down the mistress's temperature,
The night gone down memory lane,
Turning me innocently insane,
Or maybe do not know the pretense of feign,
The fever gone forever,
My sought after heart forgotten forever,
Forgiving the act of measuring the temperature,
Forgiving the self-saying sorry for ever,
Withdrawn to herself she forgot the fever.
That night she had fever,
The light house stood in mute silence erect forever,
Watching the mermaids visiting the sea shore,
Waiting since time immemorial like the immortal lover.

....

(344)

Oh! Nature

....

The mystic clouds across the horizon,
The green hills decked with the river amazon,
The clouds in motion kissing the clouds of the horizon,
Nature's opulence showing the tall green pine plantation,
The flora, fauna & mountains looking velvet green,
Droplets of rain on the green leaves
with tiny water bulbs scene,
Scenic horizon with white clouds
gliding into the forestry green,
Between the cleavages of the clouds a thin ray of sun,
Spraying radiant beams into the tiny
water bulbs for fantastic fun,
Glorifying the enigmatic nature's color in fusion,
The ecstasy of the fusion touching the soul for a boon,
The soulful presentation of the nature setting the tune,
Singing songs of the nocturnal
creature's with a beautiful tone,
Mesmerizing atmosphere paying
soulful tributes to the creation,

The magnanimous creator's magnificent expression,
Flora, fauna & flowers saluting life, love & fortune...
To amass into opulence of the greatest creation...
Soliciting love birds to chirp with their
soulful tweeters & rendition...
The soulful renditions orchestrated
beautifully into joyous version...
Gratitude of abundance flow like the immortal ocean...

. . . .

(345)

What me?

....

What me,
What you,
When we are one,
What me what you,
The me & you,
Just inseparable,

....

(346)

The Bond of friendship

....

As one sails in the time's ship,
Many crossroads of friendship,
Some signaling green some red,
A friend in need is a friend in deed,
A true friend is all weather friend,
Sharing one's woes to one's happiness,
Stands like a rock for all seasons,
Like a weather proof jacket,
Who encloses you like the bracket?
Protecting you from the evil,
Protecting you from the devil,
The true friends always stand on the anvil,
In their absence you always feel,
True friends are pearls in a bead,
Counting the beads one by one fulfilling the friends need,
The soulful bonding keeps brooding,
The soul cries insolently for the bonding,
Seeking praying for the friends wellbeing,
Happy friendship day my friends,
For standing beside me on all occasions of needs,
My heart bows down with respect
at your committed deeds.

....

(347)

Between the stifles & throttles...

....

When the soul stifles,
The Breathe throttles,
Beautiful stifles,
Throttling to choke,
When you are contained,
Within the circumference of your soul,
You are contented,
The soul breathes peace,
Breathes positive vibes.
My woes tress-pass their limits,
My happiness surpasses all altitudes,
The longitudes of stifles,
The latitudes of the throttles.

....

(348)

Bad Luck..

Why it happens to me,
Half dreamt dreams deserted,
Ruminate over the matter feeling shattered,
Why? Why? The question,
The fate's cruel abnegation,
The questioning mind,
In no mood to understand,
In no mood to accept,
The face of defeat,
Frustrating thoughts,
Hangovers of the bite,
The poison slowly spreading in,
Slowly take life to its possession,
The soul in sheer confuse,
Running amok for little solace,
Solace nowhere shows its face,
Even glasses of water can't give peace,
The revolting mind in no moods to compromise,
However time flies by giving a kiss,
Do not know how to end the turbulence,
The turbulence does not finish,
Oh! God please give me peace.
Give me little peace.

(349)

What life knows?

Life knows,
It's woes,
It's bows,
It's arrows,
Life knows
It's tears,
It's fears,
It's lows,
It's highs,
Life knows,
It's gains,
It's losses,
It's trusts,
It's faiths,
Little realizing,
That one day,
Life leaves,
Leaves for the beyond,

From the point of no return,
Still every day,
There is a chase,
War for survival,
Running a race,
For survival,
The order of the universe,
Survival of the fittest,
A gospel truth,
A compulsive faith,

. . . .

(350)

Hopeless dreams

....

Now when I see your picture,
Drawing sketches of your imaginary figure,
Imagining those moments of treasure,
Those lost moments held in the enclosure,
Measuring the depth of love for each other,
Time & tide waited for none,
We were mere lovers already done,
The catapult of time snatched you from me,
Leaving me in the youth of life,
You became the mistress of some stranger,
Separated from you forever,
Only flashbacks of your memories,
Hunt me down memory lane unlocking the treasuries,
Brooding over the past emotional encounters,
Smoking cigar after cigar burning the soul's amber,
Memory's story of pain & pleasure,
Dance before the eyes between the galaxies of stars,
As I try to touch a glowing star,
It vanishes in moments wounding me with a lifelong scar,

My aspirations remain repudiated,
The list of rejection goes abetted,
Helplessly surrender to the stretcher of destiny,
A silent war of revolt still fought like a mutiny.
Life's gimmicks has many surprises in store,
Time does not heal the wounds written on the whore,
Dark robes of the dark corridors only hunt life's shore,
Until death snatches have to suffer sipping the torture...

....

(351)

Surrendering to Thee

My surrendering to solitudes,
Enlarges the world of my loneliness,
Beliefs of nothingness encroach the mind,
Languishing in the corner of life in grind,
All worldly attachments projecting fake,
The nihilistic philosophy of nothingness,
Caught in between thoughts of being & nothingness,
Groping in the abandoned corners of darkness,
Trying to catch a glimpse of hope in harness,
But work without hope goes draws no sense,
Hope without an object faces death in the harness,
The be is being,
Not to be is nothing,
Anyone who can explain me the being,
Anyone who can define what is nothing,
In my utter helplessness surrender to thee,
With hope of the beacon amidst the groping darkness...

(352)

The Blind & Deaf existence

I know he is deaf.
I know he is blind.
In his blindness
His existence,
In his deafness,
He lives,
But with our eyes & ears open,
We fail to see,
We fail to listen,
Even avoid the ugliest scenes,
Even avoid the ugliest words,
In his world he breathes peace,
In his world he feels his self in no crisis.
Seeing a speeding vehicle we cross the road,
Hearing the blaring horns we cross life,
Life such mysterious road,
On one side of the road life,
Beyond the cross road no life.
Can't put one step back one step forward,
In broad day light even a blind girl has no say,
She feels so unsafe even to eke out a life for herself,

The eyes behind the spectacles see beyond,
Never deciphering between the evil & good,
Still better than the eyes & ears,
Blessed that does not see the tortuous words,
Blessed that does listen the tortuous tongues.
This is life the difference between
the have's & the have not's,
Here the have's lack the basic values of life,
Forget about the have not's bereft of things.

....

(353)

The Buffoons premise

One does not know himself,
However one boasts to have known the self,
The enigma remains shrouded,
Shrouded since time immemorial,
When one does not know the self,
How does one boast of proudly to know the self?
A false imaging,
A false assertion,
A false assumption,
A false presumption,
A false premise,
On which life surmises,
Life never knows the self,
It is not a physical selfie,
Clicked for possession,
Looks satisfying as long as one only sees,
But little introspection,
Thought for a moment,
Discover real self,
Then why this disbelief,
Whether I am me or not,

Wondering at the acts done,
Never thought,
Never to have done,
This is man,
Never knows the self,
Sheer bluff & buffoon of life.
Always living in illusions,
Distracted visions,
Pretty little knowing the self,
How false existence is,
Fake existence is,
Just one prick of a thorn,
Life is gone,
Boasting still to have known the self...
The false pride of the prejudiced self...

....

(354)

The Childhood feasts

. . . .

The childhood feasts,
Eggs were currying,
In cauldron full of hot water,
The egg was struggling for little gravy,
The mouth buds smelling the hot boiled eggs,
Floating elliptic images of the eggs,
Boiled rice, egg curry & tomato paste,
Mouth-watering dishes to taste,
The childhood dreams,
Each one got a palm full of rice,
Each one got one egg from house,
It was a children festival,
Celebrated with kerosene lamps,
Ovens dug on the earth,
Boiling the rice to the curry in hurry,
The children anxiously waiting hungry,
Happily rejoicing with the stomach,
Rice & the curry smelling fishy,

The tingling taste of the tomato paste,
Gulped & swallowed in absolute haste,
The banana leaf plates,
Serving the delicacies,
The children enjoying the culinary,
A childish simple mind,
Playing childish gimmicks of the kind...

....

(355)

The Assassination

. . . .

No one could see,
In broad light there was darkness,
Life was throttled in duress,
No rescuers but ants,
When the lifeless body turned to a corpse,
The ants made a bee line,
The street dogs to vultures,
Invited to the odor,
The decomposed body,
Lie there lifeless,
The Flesh eaters rejoicing,
With the vultures to the street dogs,
Relishing their stomach with a sumptuous lunch,
Sumptuous lunch till the dinner arrived,
In darkness the last remains,
Pulled the carcass into the jungle terrain,
By jackals & foxes who loved the remains,
Only the remains of the skeletal bones,
Dismantled frames lie here & there,

The weaker of the carnivores,
Just smelled the odor smelling from a distance,
Some just reveled with a piece of the bone,
No one could know,
No one saw,
Where the huge format is gone,
Yesterday's pride gone with the prejudice,
The story of pride & prejudice,
Capturing the lost pages of dice.
No one could see,
In broad day light there was darkness...

....

(356)

The Beautiful Hook...

....

Books just hook,
Capturing the human mind to cook,
Read & cook,
Cook the culinary,
Cook the delicacy,
Of the weird wild mind,
The emotions of the wisdom,
Expressed fathom,
To the domain of the soul,
In true regale,
An imprint copied,
An imprint pasted,
On eternity at the pasture,
Like the gardener pruning the plants,
The readers express their feelings pruned,
Tuned to the self with its unique combine,
Thoughts packed with ideologues,
Hacking the soul remembering the dialogues,

Remnants of the relics left on the platform,
Bringing the relics into the pages in form,
Shaping a story book,
The syntax of the words hook,
Hypnotizing the reader's mood,
Taking years & years of memories to brood,
The memoirs of the book have a captive hook...

....

(357)

The Hangman's Noose,

. . . .

The Hang-man's noose,
The tongues just ooze,
Out of the throttle,
Out of stifle,
The rope of tight-hold,
The breathe in tight fold,
The hang-man's profession,
A riddle for the human,
The hangman too a man,
Obeys the commands of another man,
Becomes a professional hangman,
Waiting years for a culprit to face death,
The sentence pronounced to be hanged till death,
The pouncing rope's tightened noose,
Stops the breathe with tongue in ooze,
The stale looks of the eyes,
As if hope in the last minute lost its vibes,
The culprit's irony,
A victim of the action committed in ignominy,

In momentary moods of frenzy,
Sentences him to the gaol to face the hinge,
To confirm death slash the vein,
To confirm & write the Death book,
The doctor pronounces him dead,
The hangman's noose,
Tightens around the neck for the tongue to ooze,
The hangman's deeds condoned,
Duty is his religion.

....

(358)

The Stimuli of the Cerebral Domain...

. . . .

The cerebral paradise,
Stimuli of thoughts in rise,
Cells multiplying in praise,
When the paradise was lost,
It lost everyone's trust,
Thoughts were jailed,
The freedom of speech failed,
When the paradise regained,
All the trusts were gained,
Amassed to opulence,
The cerebral paradise,
A man's tryst with destiny,
A mini marathon race of mutiny,
Lifelong the stimuli of direction,
Directed the limbs to function,
The invisible directed the eyes to see,
The ears to listen,
The invisible directed the mouth,
To speak,
Chew,
Eat,

The nose to breathe,
The stomach to digest,
The abdomens to process,
Filter the food,
Filter the blood,
Filter the water,
The lower abdomen,
Sprang into action,
Winding the intestines,
To pass,
The water to pass,
Excess of water to leave the body,
The hands to do multiple actions,
The legs to walk run...
The wisdom of the cerebral domain...

....

(359)

The Silent Worlds

....

In silent worlds,
We stood,
Pelting our glances,
We brood,
In silent words,
We understood,
You hitting me,
Clutching my fingers,
In your hold,
Signaling me,
To feel the pulse,
The racing beats,
In golden silence,
Feel the beats,
That was beating for me,
The evening was leaving,
Night was drawing its curtains,
You wanted to leave for home,

Loosening the grips,
Never wanted to leave,
But with capsules of emotions,
Emotions in motion,
The tears from the eye's corner,
Flowing non-stop drenching the parlor,
Silently withdrawing,
Withdrawing to ignominy,
Ignominy of the atmosphere,
We left each-other's fold,
Back to casual hold,
In silent words expressed in bold,
Slowly withdrew leaving the hold.

....

(360)

The Violet Rose...

. . . .

The violet rose,
Droplets on petals,
Asking a question,
To the questioning mind,
Does it really exist?
The blind faiths,
Of existentialism,
Does It really exist?
Betraying the truth,
The violet rose,
Does It really exist?
The mysterious exist,
Shrouded in mist,
Does it really exist?

. . . .

(361)

No day... No Night...

A poet has no day,
No night,
Day till the night,
The poet lost in his write,
Even if it is midnight,
Burn the midnight,
Plucking the sweet thought,
From the Dreams in flight,

(362)

The Annoying Effects

....

The invisible hand protects,
The visible openly betrays,
In the control of the invisible,
A different experience with the visible,
Man always remains a proposer,
God always plays the disposer,
Man with his little wisdom behaves a propeller,
God always play the role of a dispeller,
What man thinks are beyond his control,
What hides from vision's rich proves to feel,
The hide & seek game that life plays with,
The catalysts of life truly reward the breathe,
The cataclysm philosophy disturbs the psyche,
The universe stifles with the smokes belched,
Smokes belched out of the human environment,
Beating the nature destroying the eco system,
Annihilating the surrounding in our selfish aim,
War torn universe with warring minds,
The cruel sagas written by the destiny,
Disturbs the root of existence,
The invisible hand just protects,
The visible just displays annoying effects...

....

(363)

An Ounce of the Trance

Just once,
Enough in the ounce,
A just beautiful trance,
A treasured pounce,
An ounce of the trance,
Tranquil pranks,
Solitude dance,
Frowning eye brows,
Racing palpitations,
Order of the selves,
Fusion in beautiful trance,
Ounce of affection,
The wishes behave like slaves,
Surrendering to the tan,
Infinite wishes of garlands,
The guest of the mind,
Honoring the princess,
Shaking shivering with the touch,
Heart in wild emotion,
Soul in moods of creation,
Love in moods of fusion,
The ambient moonlit balcony,
The slanted rays feel drunken,
Twinkling planets
Smiling in the faraway galaxy,
The galaxy of happiness,
Twinkling brightness,

Quivering the chemistry,
Into evanescence silence,
Evanescence grace,
In the welter of doubts,
Life still sprouts,
Exhilarating dreams,
Never dreamt of,
Never thought of,
An accidental coincidence,
Often comes,
Time & again touching
Pyramids of the silence,
Burning the passions
In the rays of moonlit bathing,
Mind inviting the moon,
To take umbrage
In the soul's grace,
In the graceful silence,
Clothes only cover to hide,
But the hidden nature takes over,
Surrendering to the drunken amber.
.Just once,
one ounce of the pounce,

....

(364)

The palpable kicks,

....

The fetus moves,
Inside the wombs,
Giving feels of the awesome kicks,
Leaves the imprints unseen with divine kiss,
The mom in true regale,
Asks the dad to feel,
Palpable feelings of love,
The blood connects to the trove,
The gimmick of waiting plays baffling,
The bloated world can't sustain in trifling,
Wait for your day my lovely fetus,
Just step out of sachet,
When your time comes,
Our anxious minds wait to welcome,
Waiting for the first alarms of your cries,
Anxieties piling up for a feel of the first cries,
First born,
First child,
First cries,
Echoing in the heart,
Beating the pulse with treat,
The couple's divine ordination,
For a hold of the little creation,

Own call it our own,
Our own creation,
Our own production,
The invisible producer,
Directing the couples to be seducers,
Seducing the couple to each other,
Creating the first production,
Laying the foundation for the first creation,
Waiting for the alarms of the first cries,
Love's labor never goes waste,
Delivering the boon,
The couple's most prized possession,
The fetus moves to life,
Obeying the laws of evolution,
Obeying the divine ordination,
Sacred nature's precious creations...

. . . .

(365)

The Seasons

....

The dry heats of summer cracking the earth,
The earth experiences feelings of near death,
Even nature changes with the season's last breathe,
With the death of summer rains show up their face,
Breathing life into the thirsty appetite
of the earth's parched face,
With the death of rain comes the autumn,
The autumn brings clear blue skies with reflecting heaven,
The end of autumn gives birth to winter,
In winters chilling atmosphere life
warms up with camp fires,
Once winter bids a goodbye spring
breathes back life into the nature,
Nature behaves drunken with hypnotizing atmosphere,
The disguise of time wears a blanket of camouflage,
Changing its colors with new feather's worn to change,

....

(366)

The Arduous Journey...

A difficult road,
An arduous journey,
Walking towards uncertainty,
The blind pursuits,
Blind thoughts,
Fear echoing,
Sounds of uncertainty,
Traversing across,
The thorny path,
Thorns pricking,
Throughout the journey,
The thorns of rose,
The thorns of the cactus,
The nails of the rusted iron,
Rusted grilles of the soul,
Just crumbling,
Breaking the faith,
Breaking the trust,
Breaking the beats of the breathe,
That stifles to breathe,
How can life sustain,
The onslaught of uncertain,
The shadows of the pain,
The disguise of falsehood in hood,
The sands of no faith,
Flew the castles,
Built on sands,

The philosophy of life,
Fragile mortality,
Striking on the morale,
The morality of the tides,
They just visit,
Just recede,
None could fathom,
Accede to succumb,
Succumbing to the atmosphere,
Dragging the soul,
Withdrawn into the cocoon,
Cocoon of the possession,
The emotions of just possessed,
Life on the anvil,
Asking for the death bill,
None deciphering the veil,
The veil of the curtain,
Lifted to fail,
An abstract concept,
Difficult to accept,
The arduous journey,
On the difficult road so thorny,

....

(367)

She matters...

. . . .

She is the she,
The mama,
The Mom,
The beautiful dame,
The fairy queen of home,
The pillar of home,
The strength of the dome,
In the mental bonds binds the family to roam,
Peace & happiness for the family her dreams,
From the day she has stepped in she screams,
In her screams she retires,
In her screams her satires,
Not this not that not there,
Do not go anywhere,
Do not go near fire,
Do not go near water,
Stay sings the family choir,
The group must sing happiness round the hour,
Must take the challenge of life to cover,
The dreams of mine,
In control of thine,
Sacrificial emblem of time,
In her silent songs ceaseless pantomime,

. . . .

(368)

When the Heart is afire...

When the Heart is afire,
Expression of the awesome ire,
Fire in the ire,
Semblance of anger,
Emotional satire,
Douse the fire,
When she adores the love with prayer,
The prayer is heard,
Surrendering to the beloved gimmicks,
The gimmicks of touch & vanish,
The touches leave beautiful imprints,
Leaving shadows of the footprints,
When time recoils,
Memories just uncoil,
Renewing the faith,
Revering the trust,
Rejoicing the imprints,
Just within the closed eye lids silence,
Innumerable wishes wrought,
Touch & vanish,
Sadism in love,
Playing the tortuous trove,

In the domes of fortune,
Resides the love's fortune,
A sweet kiss implanted on the cheek of time,
Remnants of which breathlessly sighing,
Just another implant,
Another sigh,
Sighs of the beloved's roving eyes,
Sighs from the beloved's romantic fries,
Unique faith of unison,
Bliss in union,
Knocking the doors of time,
Hey, time where are you gone?
Make a comeback,
With the roving hand of the clock
Rewind back.

....

(369)

Subconscious Wisdom...

Words of wisdom,
Senses retire into the subconscious,
The Fathomless depth of the subconscious,
Even death dare touch,
Bewildered tentacles,
Beyond the spectacles,
On the slates of the retina,
The retina only painting images,
Of the surreal universe,
Melting into shadows of oblivion,
The horizon of mind,
Feelings of bliss in kind,
Words of wisdom,
Knowledge is a huge dome,
Peace steps to alight,
From the galaxy of the flight,
Wisdom taking umbrage,
Shelter in grace,
For true rejoice,
For true solace,
Words of wisdom,
Renewing the faiths of the dome...

(370)

River's flowing into the ocean...

....

The river flows into ocean,
Earth carries the water in one direction,
In the ocean's direction,
No one ever dug the river's direction,
Nature's magic spade cutting the routes towards the ocean,
The ocean waits for the river in its shores,
The tides of the rivers swell into the ocean's chorus,
Mingling into the salted waters the sweetness,
The thirsty ocean drinking aplenty to appease,
The thirst of the centuries,
Hidden inside the ocean's treasuries,
The gems hidden inside the cocoon's cell,
Inside the abysmal cocoon of the mill,
The receding tides welcome the river's virgin waters,
That comes sailing from the heavens,
Swimming through the curvy mountains,
Touching the flora fauna of the jungles wilderness,
Nature noted watching in absolute silence,

Portraying the dreams of innocence,
Carrying the filtered waters in opulence,
Flourishing aside the hutments with villages,
Thatched roofs sheltering innocent
people under its hilly cleavages,
Beyond the spectacular woods a heaven exists,
The dreams of the ancient civilizations
comes with their tales,
The river flowing since time immemorial
with symbolic opulence,

....

(371)

Seeking an Eternal Explanation...

....

The ship sinks into the ocean,
With the crew & the captain,
The captain's life jacket sunken,
The captain never could feel,
A captain above who sails life's vessels,
The captain's ego was the reason for the block,
Hitting the vessel against the Inchcape rock,
Splinters of the ego giving a rude shock,
The waves hitting against the rock,
Passion since time immemorial with the sea & the rock,
Mad attraction of sea in turbulence
hitting against the rock,
Saving itself from the nature's fury and tidal shock,
The tsunami that wrought havoc hitting against the rock,
The best healer (time) will tell the saga
of hitting against the rock,
One only bleeds with life breathing a life time shock,
Little realizing that hitting against Inch-cape rock,
Writing a wound betrays,

The action turning a nightmare into rude shock,
With the crew, captain & the ship too sink,
Sleep walking within the resenting heart's wink...
Pride & ego temporary possessions,
The actions of destiny betrays often,
With every action an equal & opposite reaction,
The eternal question often seeking an explanation...

....

(372)

The Fiesta of Happiness..

....

Marriages are made in heaven,
Men & women mere performers,
The entire world is a stage,
All men & women mere players,
Mimicking the divine evolution,
Mimicking the laws of emotion,
A beautiful atmosphere charged in motion,
The two in one,
Soulful motion,
Moments in moon,
Moments in fusion,
Infusing energy of passion,
The Adam's apple a mad attraction,
Who so ever has eaten?
Resilient into frenzied moods of attraction,
Even for fraction of a moment lovely fusion,
Passion garlanding the soul into a beautiful prison,
A beautiful bonding illusion,
A beautiful body bath of the seasons,
The fiesta of happiness of true reasons,

Sighing like a furnace,
The flames blasting in to awesome embrace,
Embezzlement of properties,
To a beautiful propriety,
Making sense smell the sensuous,
The sizzling sprinkling foaming of the passionate fumes,
Breathing sensuously soul's undisclosed romances,
Ruminating over the beautiful fragrance,
X factors soliciting into a beautiful transfusion...
Paying the moments the price of true oblivion...

....

(373)

The Caravan of Time

The sands of time,
Beautiful to rhyme,
A beautiful pantomime,
Countless ordeal time just flies by,
Leaving traces of its impeccable sighs,
In the emerald gold of the quiet land,
The whispers of the desert's invisible wand,
The pulse of the desert searching the lost strings,
The isolated desert's master,
Lost in the swallowing aftermath,
Under the embrace of slumber,
Just dreaming to be queen of the desert,
Little knowing the master's whims,
Master's moods,
When the whips & lashes,
Would bring her to senses,
OMG my master do not be harsh,
Stop your whips & lashes
Leave me to race,
Track down the soul left behind,
Before the deserts sand's settle in kind,

Tracing the footprints left on the sands of time,
For one cardinal truth since birth of time,
Traces & footprints live till death of time,
Soul's immortality hides in the infinity of time,
Time a beautiful testimony,
Soul's secret never reveals,
The sands of time,
A beautiful pantomime,
A beautiful whispering rhyme,
Echoing eternally the innocence of time,

....

(374)

The Whispering Echoes...

....

The Whispering Echoes of the snail's pace...
Baring opens the secrets of existence,
The shelter home,
The snail's dome,
Hiding from nature,
Under the tiny pink mushroom hutment,
A live hutment of ephemeral existence,
Still the snail's hard shell,
The soft face of snail sprouts out,
In falling rainy showers taking a bath,
Bath of the glistening hard shell,
The horns with the face withdrawn
into the cocoon of the shell,
The cell inside the shell,
Breathing life of the seasonal existence,
With rains born,
Without nectars of the season,
Life has no reason,
The bleeding nature's rainy season,
Soaking the earth flora, fauna & the snail,
The snail in regale,
Displaying a shining spectacle,
Sprouting occasionally from the cocoon of the shell,
The retina paints a beautiful picture of the vision,
On the canvass of the rainy season,
The oil paint of the watery structure
of live shell with a reason,

The stony bed of the earth heaving a sigh of relief,
The stony hard surface does not soak,
The dry cells of the metallic spill just break,
The earth searching the pores for little freak,
Soaking it to sprout the embryo of
the mushroom seed to creep,
Creep through the pores of the hard
rock to see light to peep,
Take a glimpse of the seasons eternal showers,
Soak in the infinity of the raining
speeds of the nature's gears,
The sheltered shell under the pink
canopy mushroom home,
Breathing life at snail's pace in its ephemeral dome,
The snails shell blissfully seeking little freedom,
The mesmeric powers of divinity,
From a snail to man providing the cute freedom,
The cute little freedom in the planet's echoing dome,
The echoes of freedom,
Peace,
Love sung at snail's pace from the infinite home,

....

(375)

The Wreaths pledged...

....

Wreaths pledged through the poetic symphonies,
But life is never a poetry book for
hunger stricken universe,
Unfurling the tricolor of India,
The tricolor we salute,
The orange white & green,
With the wheel of the 24 spokes in between,
The heart bleeds with reverence,
To the great souls who did the sacrifice,
Today celebrating freedom,
Even with an empty stomach the space
confuses the meaning of freedom,
Fighting hungers for the little freedom,
Freedom the birthright,
Does not define the meaning of the right,
Beggars beg before the temple,
While devotees beg inside the temple,
The sad irony someone begging the freedom from hunger,
Someone begging for opulence,
The freedom for the milieu,
Freedom through non-violence,
Does not perceive the true meanings of freedom,
Because of the presence of hunger,
Hunger bitten,
Poverty stricken,

The subject of the ruling,
The erstwhile rulers to the present,
Still lost in searching the meaning of freedom,
A free will,
A free diction,
A free space,
Free lights,
Free water,
Still lack the freedom,
Freedom from darkness,
Freedom from hunger,
Freedom of peace,
The society needs to revamp its looks,
The unfurling the tricolor,
Rescue the sufferers in darkness who
know no meaning of the freedom

....

(376)

The Shy Giggles..

. . . .

In your shy giggles,
Beautiful moustache tickles,
Through the giggling.
As I flutter away,
The moustache
Mistaken to be a butterfly,
But memories of Charlie Chaplin,
Embrace the giggles,
Irresistible smiles,
Irresistible sighs,
The pulse feeling beaten,
Between faster to slow rhythms,
Only if you can feel,
My soul sure shall feel,

. . . .

(377)

Symphonies from the cocoons of a butterfly...

Today Butterflies in my dreams,
In my poems,
I just can't understand,
Why the butterflies on the garden of my mind,
Whenever I see a butter fly,
I run with my lenses behind the fly,
It always eludes saying bye,
I feel shattered,
Back to my senses battered,
But butterflies only triggered me,
My inner talent of writing expressing the real me,
Never looked back ward since then,
In all probability rediscovered my talents hidden,
One after the other followed the passion,
Writing poems with invisible oblivion,
The beautiful butterflies reign,
In my poetic symphony's domain
The ephemeral butter fly,
An imprint in the soul saying bye...

(378)

Ecstasy of the mind...

....

Ecstasy in the form,
Woven dreams just roam,
For little romance,
For little unison in trance,
The trance of the moment in physical oblivion,
Laws of evolution a creative passion,
The mental aberration,
Leading to physical consummation,
Blushing at the truth at times,
Confessions take recourse to silent miles,
The poetic expression,
A passionate depiction,
The invisible connection,
Compels a poet to written passion,
In his poems hides the real sarcasm,
In his poetic forms hides the mediaeval form...

....

(379)

The Frozen Dreams

....

Snows of the winter form ice,
Bonding with the winter's chilling freezes,
Roads to trees wear the attires,
The mirror of winter beautifully reflects,
Nature's frozen dreams,
Gravity's rainbows,
Winter's rich characters show up,
The season's depth greets the planet's hope,
The planet's blanket of snows,
Amazes the survivor's with nature's chilling blows,
Old men freeze to death,
Suffocating to breathe,
Nature has its seasonal character,
The planet has to teach behavior,
Renewing the faith of the director,
The director hiding inside the incubator,
When the season washes the planet with its frown,
The season continues in harness during its incubation,

The incubator processes the seed with its warmth-ness,
When winter's child bakes inside during the process,
The season has its childhood,
Its adulthood,
Death comes with burning wood,
The season's reign comes to end,
When spring takes the turn & nature's blend,

………………………………………………

(380)

Just Hold your Breath,

....

Hold your breath,
Leave your breathe,
Take a long breathe,
Slowly leave the long breathe,
Move the abdomen,
Move the intestine,
Just stand up,
Bend forward,
Touch your toes,
Move your joints,
Exercise every joint,
Rotate first clockwise,
For five times,
Rotate anticlockwise,
For five times,
From toes to fingers,
Rotate all joints,
Close your eyes,

Invoke east,
Invoke south,
Invoke west,
Invoke the north,
Invoke the guru,
Chant Om inside,
Life is yoga,
Yoga life,
Exercise for fitness,
Exercise for wellness,

. . . .

(381)

The Boon of monsoon

The bride of monsoon,
Arrives in the month of June,
Wets the parched earth,
The dry earth fills in quenching the thirst,
The parched soil soaks to unite,
Seeds left behind start to germinate,
The farmer moves with his yokel,
After the soil is wet to depth,
The farmer ploughs the earth,
The seeds are sown,
Nurseries grown,
When rains pour enough,
Plantation takes place with faith,
The season's downpours,
Giving life, love & passion to the seeds,
The panicles pregnant with corn,
Wait for the rains to leave,
The produce comes in abundance,
The year's produce for granary's vacant space,

The granary's mines mine them inside,
Feel them with the warmth of the soil,
The straw stocked for the cattle feed,
The straw covers the soiled houses with their reed,
The bride of monsoon,
A blessing in disguise of a boon,
From animals to flora, fauna & the jungle,
Thirst of every soul quenched to the angle,

. . . .

(382)

The Mountaineer,

....

Threw the rope to hold,
Hold the hill,
In its clutch,
Climbing the arduous,
Rocky paths,
Really an uphill task
An amateur,
Not an astute rock climber,
The hills were beautiful,
Flora & fauna to plantations,
Was my companion?
Throughout the trek,
Climbed without break,
Reach the altitude of the hill,

....

(383)

The Crescent Moon

. . . .

The moon in crescent,
Smiles radiant,
The slow rhythms,
Of the evening,
Stepping out of the galaxy,
Shadows of the fox,
A long shadow in the tracks,
The echoes of the footsteps,
Imprints of the shadows,
Cloudy faint ambience,
Seeking of the seeker,
The seeker knoweth the sought,
The seeking knows the crescent,
The evening is just present,
Carrying rhythms of the radiant,
Faint visions of the ambient,
Composition from the didactic poetry,
Imagining minds in tryst,

Show of pure magnanimity,
Spreading opulence of equanimity,
Equating the atmosphere with opportunity,
Bliss in tryst with destiny,
Blissful serenity,
Bathing the soul of humanity,
A child to an adult all feeling the vanity,
The Vanity fair's reflective beams of purity,
Purifying the soul to radiance within it...
The moon in crescent,
Smiling at the radiant,
The beams comforting the vibrant thoughts...

....

(384)

Petals in Passion...

....

Entwined,
Petals of passion,
Love at times plays ransom,
The ravaging ransom,
Bruising the soft petals,
The soft tender branches,
The soft tender lips,
The rose buds smiling at the honey bees,
Whispering in the ears of the honey bees,
Suck Oh! Honey bee as much as you can,
Carry my pollens as much you can,
My petals I dedicate to you,
Your stings you dedicate to me,
In the sacrifice promises kept,
Lovely promises left,
With the dreams of theft,
The beauty of the bodies lift,

Burgled treasures,
Hissing pleasures,
The burgled pleasures,
Histrionics sizzlers,
Sipping the nectars,
The nectars bathing the petals,
Bathing the bodies,
In the river of histrionics,

....

(385)

Oh! Mind you is a wonderful chameleon

. . . .

Mind is a wonderful chameleon,
Changing its colors often,
Season after season,
When comes the rain,
She grows green,
When comes the autumn,
She grows yellow unseen,
Nature's divine ordination,
A beautiful chameleon a true kin,
In the green world of nature,
She is a treasure,
In the autumnal migration,
Camouflaging migration,
The laws of self-protection,
Endowed being born,
The stomach becomes the reason,
The sachet to be filled in,
Surviving amidst the danger,
A green forest is the best wear,
Branches hiding the lovely creature,

Ambush her weapon,
Prey her only intuition,
Hunger of procreation,
A natural compulsion,
The law of evolution,
Magnanimous chameleon,
A harmless friend of nature,
Echoing the smiles of the creature,
In my heart's she resides,
Nature's laws she abides...
Oh! You are a wonderful chameleon,
Change the natural motion,
Without change life becomes moron,
Oh! Mind you are a wonderful chameleon...

....

(386)

The Nature seduces

The irony of life,
Even a centipede,
A cricket,
A soil worm,
Struggles,
To eke out life,
The ant is an exception,
The honeybees,
The micros truly amazing,
The macros truly puzzling,
The rainfly,
Before the rain comes,
Ambush the atmosphere,
Dance with droplets,
Clip there wings,
That is life,
Sail away with the rains,
The termites,
Excellent home makers,
In day they build their empires,
The mountains,
They say it is a store house,
The chain of ant's store,

Food stuff for inclement weather,
For seasons they store,
The queen termite,
Reigns the kingdom,
Their lifestyle,
A short span,
An ephemeral existence,
Their days of mating,
In twinkle of eye,
Lay eggs,
In matters of hours,
Their off springs on the den,
The snake's speed,
A scared breed,
Mate in seasons,
Lay their wrappers,
Go to hibernation,
Lay their eggs inside a burrow,
The olive ridley,
Lays innumerable eggs,
Finds a warm place,
Under the sands,
Near the sea,

The street dogs,
When comes the mating season,
Openly seduce the partner,
Laying the breeds,
Time is the spacing,
For a centipede,
To a butterfly,
To a snake,
To a honeybee,
To a dog,
To man,
All a divine ordination,
The nature's obligation,
The laws of evolution,
Creation & procreation.
Natural seduction....
The amazing equation,
For centipedes,
Short span,
Short live short breed,
For a human it is a miracle,
Needs no description...

. . . .

(387)

Wahl! Wahl! Showman...

The celestial showman,
Hides in invisible tan,
The natural process of seduction,
Animals just live for procreation,
Eking out life for creation,
The herbivore universe,
Amazing opulence,
The green grass to trees,
For herbivore consumption,
The carnivore universe,
A word of terse,
Killing is their passion,
The survival of the fittest,
The natural food chain,
One eating the others being eaten,
The gifted qualities,
The herbivore harmless,
Non-violent in manners,
The carnivore harm-full,
Violent in manners,
Herbivores preach peace,
Peaceful co-existence,
Carnivores no option,
Hunting & killing the passion,

Nature's food chain,
Balance in magnificent equation,
The carnivore kills its prey,
For stomach full of digestion,
The herbivore world,
Opulence is the word,
No shortage of food,
Plants to rely on the soil,
The air, water & soil,
Fill their existential role,
An invisible plan,
Struggling human,
Since time immemorial,
To unravel the equation,
Wahl! Wahl! The celestial showman,
Executing round the clock an invisible plan...
Wah...Wah SUPERMAN...

....

(388)

Lost in the Vast Space of Time...

Leaving that evening on the shore,
We wrote our promises on tear,
When a mild storm blew,
With the receding tide of time it flew,
Never again could we catch up,
Only reminders of that eve on top,
Never did we imagine ever,
The promises were forgotten & over,
In the traces of shore,
Nothing left even the tears,
Everything receded back to the ocean,
Retrieving the self for a little while often,
Trying to catch a glimpse of the thread,
Faint memories just leave me to brood,
Trying to paint your beautiful face,
Trying to write love on your beautiful grace,
Innocent wishes fake promises only feign,
Never in life came the occasion again,
Lost in the vast space of time,
Never again we remembered the chime...

(389)

The Blinking Thoughts...

Unless you sink,
In to the abysmal,
Unless you blink,
Depth of the fathomless,
Unless you think,
The tide of thoughts,
Wave of thoughts,
Do not surf on
The ocean of mind,
Oh! Mermaid of sea,
Carrying the potion of ambrosia,
Receding waves,
Kissing the beach,
Recede back,
Into the abysmal,
Depth of the ocean,
Unless you think,
Pen does not flow the ink,
Unless pen flows,
The jelly of the mental fish,
Swim in the shores,

Thoughts do not visit,
The nets with the setting sun,
The setting sun in the horizon,
Sinking into the ocean,
Creating magnificent ripples,
On the surfing tides of the ocean,
The poet keeps waiting,
For the tides to visit,
His beloved waiting at the other end of the ocean,
Radiating tides playing hide & seek,
Surfing swimming messages to the beloved,
Waiting at the end of the horizon,

....

(390)

The Chuckled Breathe...

Lurking danger,
Anvil of death near,
Far away from fear,
The fearless before the ferocious,
Surrendering in total abnegation,
When fate summons,
The weak has no option,
In the stronger's jurisdiction,
Life's ultimate truths,
Bare open before the chuckled breathes,
The last question asked in silence,
Seek the last boon the last wish,
The hangman asks the prisoner,
Moments before the tying the hanger,
The summons of destiny,
One has no choice except a silent mutiny,
The silence of mutiny,
Will leave traces of the ruin,

Before death a happy surrender,
Let the lion be the death god feasting a happy devour,
Secrets of the incomprehensible,
Difficult definition beyond the sensible,
Lurking danger,
Far away from fear,
Fearless surrender,
The being of fearless soldier,
When the enemy appears from the ambush,
In moments of camouflage the finale of finish,

....

(391)

The Vanity Fair...

A gun without barrel,
Puppet mimicries of fear,
Surrounded by Gun men,
The puppet does not know what it means,
Like a King asking a beggar,
Know me who I am?
The beggar laughs,
Yelling at you,
Look at this bugger,
Knowing not who he is?
For a pauper vanity is a shadow,
Shadow of the powerful ego,
A gun without barrel,

(392)

The Fragile Glass Wings....

....

Let us not end,
Let the conversation go on,
The poetic pen write on,
Poems of love,
Feelings of the beautiful emotional trove,
Excavating the feelings from the minds grove,
Penning down the words of love,
If half the planet could learn love,
In poetic Platonism,
Reside our faith,
Retire our trust,
Bridge the gap between man & man,
Man though born free,
Tied with a chain,
Half of the tragedies of world
Fly like the glass winged butterfly,
Propping up the mustached Charlie Chaplin's butterfly,
Let us never end,
Let us not bend,
Stand tall to the occasion,
Celebrating the moods,
Embracing in true fusion,

....

(393)

Flamingoes in the Soul's Lawn,

....

Just feeling flown,
Swimming with the fin,
Like an aquarium fish,
The morning just hiss,
Serenity of silence,
Solitude blowing peace,
Flying into ecstasy,
The dome of bliss,
The sublime chime,
Clime of the rhyme,
Symphonies mime,
Ears surrendering to climb,
The soul feeling deeper,
Songs of the fathomless rapper,
Each word spoken,
Each pause often,

A beautiful modulation,
Each whisper a turn,
Just feeling flown,
When happens the unknown,
Unthinkable oblivion,
Unseen blessings pouring in,
The innocence of petals in soul open,
Just getting flown,
The flamingoes in the soul's fathomless lawn...

....

(394)

Whines of the childhood,

. . . .

Collect the milk,
Breaking the leaf,
Collect a grass stem,
Fold it into a round,
At one corner,
Dip the round,
In the potion,
Just blow,
The thin film,
That forms,
Holding the borders,
Of the stem's round,
Around bubble,
Starts sailing,
Into the air,
Creating a miracle,
Miracle bulb,
Floating in the air,
Carrying air inside,
Sparkling rainbows,

On the bulbs surface,
The eye just wonders,
Retina innocently captures,
The captivating image,
In moments the bulb bursts,
Blow another,
One after the other,
Collecting the nectar,
A childish dreamy affair,
In a dreamland the child lives,
Living in ecstasy of the hives,
A childish dream,
Run after the fun,
Innocence of tons,

....

(395)

Erotica

. . . .

Erotic erosions,
In blissful slavery,
In sighs of sweats,
Wet passions,
Clasped clay molds,
Even carved images,
Of the stones,
Bleeding for ages,
Stories of poses,
The invisible purpose,
Teaching for civilizations,
Love is no sin,
Love is a passion,
For creation,
For procreation,
Silent carved,
Nude monuments,
Wearing vision,
For ages bathing,
With nature,
Wearing the nude
Atmosphere,
Millions of eyes,
Captivating vision,

The craftsmen,
Build the huge edifice,
In their life's sacrifice,
Priceless erotica,
Priceless artefacts,
Teaching silently,
For ages,
Love,
Life,
Passion,
Erotica,
For procreation,
Natural obligation,
Divine ordination,
Erotic erosion,

....

(396)

Mesmeric flamboyance,

. . . .

Mesmeric flamboyance,
Life flowing in abundance,
Not knowing is ignorance,
Life eternally glowing,
A river eternally flowing,
Accepting the glowing tributes,
Reciprocating the great attributes,
Nature,
Flora,
Fauna,
Insect,
To animal,
To man,
Everyone in standing ovation,
The magical universe shining,
Ever since its creation,
The dictum of procreation,
Since then,
Pastures of the blooming green lawn,
The dawn's reflective beams on the horizon,
Until dusk the flamboyant sun,
Eternally composing an unique unison,

The season's periodic plan,
Feelings of harsh summer action,
To the downpours of the rain,
Follows the beautiful autumn,
Fiestas of the festive season,
The winter coming with chilled spine,
Giving the chilled feelings to the bone,
The spring comes like a beautiful lash of the season,
Waving the branches & flowers like a dancing queen,
The cuckoo from the mango groves sings hidden,
Living creatures feeling the swift breeze feeling flown,
The flamboyance of each season,
Throws the tantrums mesmeric reign,
Magic's of eternity in reality of the run,

………………………………………………

(397)

Daffodils...

....

Oh! Daffodils
Drunken amber instills
Secret meanings in your frills,
The radiant flames just steal,
In the radiance the clouds kneel,
From across the clouds corners,
The rays of opulence behave soul turners,
Turning the ambience into heaven,
The heaven's mellows,
Lost in the beautiful yellow,
The nursery sings below,
The faraway horizon tuning beetles,
In the vacuum of serenity,
Soul beseech blessings of infinity,
Infinity to eternity,
Gift of the evanescence bounty,
Bliss of surrendered sublimity,
Submissions at the feet of beauty,
Oh! Daffodils,
Obligations of long lived dreams,
Come flowing in the realms,
Oh! Daffodils,

....

(398)

Ridiculous Deeds

The words,
The deeds,
Always differed,
The spoken words,

The written words,
The spoken words,
The written words,
Must be well crafted,

Human actions,
Human deeds,
Worried
The centuries to bleed,
The deeds never heed,
Why they did,
What they were supposed
Never to do,
Did?

The course of destiny changed,
Every word they said,
Falsity in every word,
Left every one betrayed,

The words
The deeds,
Must be crafted,
With care said,

Intent of peace,
Object of peace,
Only goal peace,
Must be honestly said,
Must be an honest deed...

....

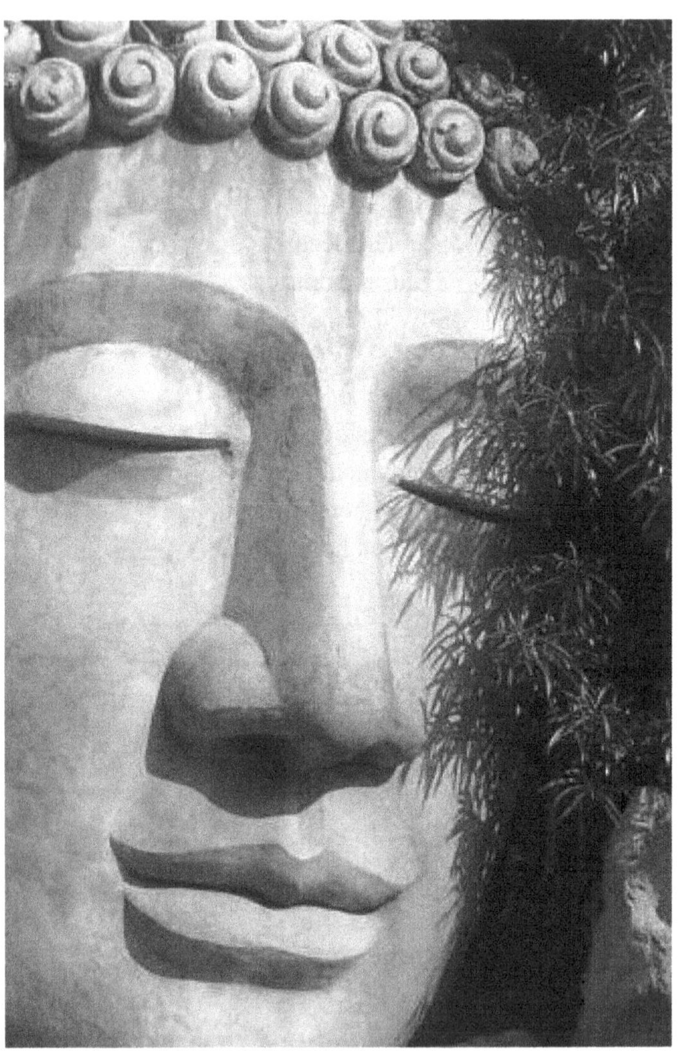

(399)

Gleaming Salvation

....

Under the Banyan tree,
Siddhartha sought enlightenment,
Enlightenment alighted,
Soulful feelings delighted,
Visions dream accomplished,
Siddhartha was enlightened,
Enlightened the world vision,
The bodhisattva philosophy,
Flowing into the confluence,
The confluence of life,
Flowing into the confluence in absolute rife,

Follow Buddha,
Follow the confluence,
The mendicant abdicating opulence,
The king abhorred the opulence,
Opulence of the kingdom,
Abdicating the peace of home,
Seeking wisdom,
The seeker knoweth the fathom,
In the depth of fathom,
In the abyss of the fulcrum,
Lies the wisdom,
A human dream,
Of the realm,
Peace to gleam,

Adoring the monkhood,
In monkhood lived the real hood,
Came with nothing Oh! Man why brood,
Committing sin after sin,
While going carry the burden,
The burden of the sin,
The caravan of sin,
The soul's regret,
Why this ferrets,
The soul's quest,
One goal one quest,
Oh! Just leave me to rest,
Rest into the silence,
Into sublime bliss,
In to symbolic heaven of peace.

....

(Buddha was an Ascetic, Bodhisattwa in
'Nirvana' which means salvation of the soul.

(400)

The Deafening Voice,

....

The recitation,
True inspiration,
My life line,
Expression,

Fin the journey of life,
A supportive fife,
Playing music of command,
Commandeering the life band,

The borders of life,
Little protective relief,
The bullets of the mouth,
Fired from the barrel of the couth,

The recited rhymes,
Voicing the pantomimes,
Heard from far away chimes,
Soul transcending to a beautiful clime,

The creator,
Knows the shelter,
Filtered clusters,
Sending the busters,

The creativity,
Passion of serenity,
The horizon's beauty,
Dawn till dusk a celebrity,

Taking a turn,
Around the axis is no fun,
The planetary position,
The earth rotates around the sun,

The sun is stationery,
The earth's rotor,
Moves like a motor,
Rotating around the planetary cluster,

The silent feeble,
Resonating vibes,
Creating the jibes,
Ignoble motives,

Rotating without a fixed point,
No genesis or crux of the sight,
In the invisibility of time a continuous fight,
Struggling to survive life's battles of fright...

Image of divinity,
Enigmatic infinity,
In letters not words hiding perfidy,
What is the divinity?

A mystery of the universe,
Think tank going perverse,
Patience playing a game of terse,
No words suit the theatre of the verse,

. . . .

(401)

Moon in the Petals Cocoon,

....

You demanded the honey from moon,
The dream of last night I told had seen,
Promising you the sweetest of honey,
Waited night long at the gates of the moon,
For my heart throbbing heroine,
My heart's weakness could be felt around,
But you did not turn up to fulfil the round,
The moon blushed at my innocence,
The moon how long could wait could feel the sense,
Slowly she moved on counting the rippling tides offence,
Hitting at the shores of love time & again reckless,
The body was submerged in moon beams,
Radiating with opulence of the waves,
Touching kissing and singing the lullabies,
The lullabies of the shore song by the ocean,
Innumerable times the mermaids knocked me down,
You were the mermaid of my dreams I crown,
No sighs in bliss of the moon beams serenade,
Amidst the unrelenting waves washing
my dream hurt facade,
The shadows of the eclipse still hunt my arcade,
Sitting at the shore of silence wait for my dream mermaid,

Like the moon one day life will leave for heaven,
If not you but will for sure carry your feelings in reign,
However you never understood your
promise was sheer feign,
Love never is at fault the Platonism
philosophy leave me blank & vein,
The sweet scars you wrote down
memory lane becomes a bane,
But a platonic lover never can curse his
beloved considering the boon,
Remembering the momentary feelings
treasured in the petals of the cocoon,
In the moon beams amber of serene cool radiance,
Blissfully my soul was busy imaging
your face from the distance....

. . . .

(402)

The Mysterious Universe,

Sitting on the shore that moonlit night,
Built the empires of love & fight,
A whiff of wind shakes the castles,
A running tide chases away us,
The foundation shaken runs away,
The tides again & again surfing the moon,
In its receding waters pulling the castle,
Back into the ocean storing the castle,
Under its fathomless house in the abyss,
Each time a castle was stolen away,
The tides were in love with the castle,
The castles were built with sand of the sea,
The sea could not spare its child in glee,
The sand belonged to the sea,
Without sand the sea can't survive,
The audacity of sea was so offensive,
We stood helpless without being defensive,
The sea was soliciting with its happiness,
Come lovers eternally for me to enjoy,

(403)

The Unknown Expeditions

. . . .

Sea & the sand can't stay apart,
In their aqua-marine universe innumerable fish,
The beautiful star fish swimming like a star,
The tiger fish sailing its black beauty,
The piranha's ensemble moving in arcade,
Radiantly glowing pride of the fins,
The dangerous shark to the huge built whale,
The Lilliput's do not understand the language but regale,
Surfers only sail on the surface of the sea,
Divers get inside the fathomless to feel the abyss,
The ignoble universe its tantrums
from the depth of the seas,
The aqua culture is a different world,
Human dreams are beyond comprehension,
Three fourth of the universe breathe aqua,
The left out one fourth breathe the gas in space,
The under-water life an enigmatic piece,

. . . .

(404)

The Alien Universe

....

Expeditions shrouded in mystery of the treasure,
Enigma of the spheres above,
Spheres under the earth,
Spheres above earth,
The atmosphere,
Stratosphere,
The biosphere,
As one traverses invisible aliens,
Invisible particles breathe universe to existence,
Under the crust of the earth,
Live the shining minerals with the black diamonds,
Half the truths of the universe beyond comprehension,
The universe remains a shrouded mystery,
More of pages open digging the history,
Pyramids to Harappa civilization,
Leave relics of the mundanely possession,
The dinosaur too lived a civilization,
Time the record keeper being watchman,
Is it the divine origination questions by default?
The mysterious universe an intellectual verse,
Truths of the realities challenging the universe,
How long NASA will take time,
To unravel the mysterious rhyme,

Only yesterday the sound of the SUN was recorded,
The sound by default echoes like the OM.
Truth of glowing furnace echoing the hum,
Before civilizations could understand,
Before civilizations could comprehend,
Time swiftly passes by into ages & ages,
From the Tretrayas,
To the Dwaparas,
To the Kaliyug (the age of war),
And finale the Satyayug (the age of truth),
The mysteries continues eluding the human verse,
The versatility, the volatility of the perverse,

....

(According to Indian Mythology there are four yuga's. Yuga is time of countless centuries where in Dwapara Lord Krishna, in Tretaya Lord Rama, in Kaliyuga the War Lords the survival of the fittest (human behavior becomes treacherous, blasphemous, liars, thieves, living in material dome, rape, torture & human slavery etc.) of one human by another and in Satya Yuga the Age of Truth where everybody speaks truth and truth reigns in all spheres.

(405)

The Histrionic Affair....

....

The sea was roaring with annoyance,
The moon on the sky was in flamboyance,
Sailing with the tides a passion of radiance,
Sailing surfing the tidal waves,
It was a full moon night,
The sea waits for the moon for the special night,
Sea & moon that night like young adolescent,
Play hide & seek showing the month long wait,

Unless the moon beams its face of radiance,
The sea does not breathe peacefully with the waves,
The waves at the sight of the moon rush shoreward,
Beating their bodies bruising against the sandy bed,
The sea sings songs of love with high roaring notes,
Flirting with the moon hiding in the fishing boats,
Innumerable lovers visit the shore offering them,
The ambience sings the song of love of within-ness,
The high tides of love flow like love of the waves,
Entwining the beloved's inside the cocoon of the troves,
Flowing back into the waters of love
the beloved's hearts throbs,
Sighs of the waves from the ocean of the soul,
The molten furnace of the radiance plays foul,
Ignorantly lovers play the game of unison in bliss,
The sea with the moon lit ambience full of smiles,
The sea too starts its high rise tides playing with the moon,

The roaring moans just recoil the
sounds with a beautiful tune,
The tall plants with long stretch of
sandy bed shake themselves,
Blown up fully with nature's hugs &
kisses of the leaves with branches,
Solitude waiting with patience with the mute light house,
Precious feels of the momentary songs of the fusion,
Caressing the beloved's long lock the
beloved moves to transfusion,
Sitting in trance of opulent flowing like the high rise tides,
The tides brushing with high sounding giggles with chides,
Fathom of love the nautical mile travelled like the ship,
The captain could never gauge the
distance travelled in flip,
The flipchart sailing the bruised
pictures of the ravaged passage,
Memoirs of the ravage written on the
sands of time with beautiful usage...
The sea was angry with the full moon
with fathomless annoyance,
Repenting at the bay waiting for the
flamboyant night's radiance....

....

(406)

When the Lava flows un-interrupt...

When the dormant volcanoes start to erupt,
The lava continues to flow un-interrupt,
The lava leaves traces of the scars of the depth,
The scars society takes times to fill with faith,
Still the atmosphere does not understand,
Leaves the situation orphan on the street to stand,
The mutiny keeps burning inside,
Least caring the destiny living beside,
This is no place to live,
This is no society to believe,
Bias of gender continue undeterred,
How long they will take to feel fettered,
How long will it take the atmosphere to change?
The universe has walked centuries believing in the being,
The being translates the difficult situation such easily,
Why not being translate the bias
with its simplicity casually,
Unless the psyche is erased from the soul of the society,
The universe wears a mute spectacle of the incident,
What happens in terror infested land?
Humanity has taken umbrage in the silence of the sand,
Dare open the dormancy,
Face the slaughter from infancy,

This is no place to surrender with your humility,
Half the universe does not understand your magnanimity,
A compulsive dormancy injected
into the mountain of mind,
The mutiny burning with molten flames of the lava inside,
Enough of the dormant sympathies
playing the symphonies,
Succumbing to the harsh beats of the
music mocking empathies,
Life never could measure its nautical miles,
Death in harness counting the bodies in the piles,
When the dormant volcanoes start to erupt,
The lava continues to flow Un interrupt,
Only traces of the scars never healing
the wounds in couth....

. . . .

(407)

Blind Love

Love is blind,
A song of the mill in the grind,
Love songs just bind,
Hearts into mind,
By default love,
Is a magic trove?
The prison can't hide the dove,
The dove talks only love,
Can't humans imitate the dove?
Spread the message of love,
The hatred from universe move,
Filling the gaps of the beauty of love,
The innocent victims be given little love,
Little pampering little patting on the back,
The blurred images in mind of the hack,
Must be erased from the mind's book,
War torn people turning mad crook,
The wound wrought on the war book,
Turns the saint to a war freak,
Long time gone since world fought,
The last war the world war two,
Thought the world enough of the fight,
If the mad modern world does not,

Learn from the past,
A human madness of the sectarian cult,
Is looming large on the community,
Will leave the world destroyed with bolt,
Oh! Humans please do not repeat the same fault,
Again & again to teach you conscience by default,
How long can you believe in the fight,
For proving the survival of the fittest,
Let us believe in the brotherhood cult,
Try our destinies re-written the cult of love,
Teaching us peace to reign in our grove,
Breathe peace, breathe love,
Sharing each other's pain & pleasure of the grove,
The universe beseeching blind love,
Blind love...the ambrosia from the dove...

....

(408)

The Whispering soul....

....

The whispers from the soul,
Sail me to the sea gull,
My wandering vision,
Loves the prison,
Prism of the vision,
The sight of the sea gull,
Solitude sailing with a lull,
Rhyming the lullabies,
Lulling the ambience like babies,
Dropping from flight,
Catching the prey in fight,
Visual imageries of sailing clouds,
The blue amber hiding in shrouds,
Rains from nowhere winking from beneath,
The clouds turning to droplets from the sheath,
Dropping on the rippling waves of the seas,
The waves with the showering rains ready for kiss,
Enjoying the rains the sea widens its broader lips,
On the broad width of the sea a storm arrives to kiss,
The aqua marine world opens its lips,
For a drop of the divine nectar falling from the heaven,
The sweet nectar of the ambrosia once in a blue moon,
Festival of nature dancing on the surfing tides of the ocean,
The nature goes wild & careless too during celebration,

The atmosphere in intoxication drinking nature's wine,
The nature's distilled droplets of rain,
Each drop of the nectar downpours
for every living creature,
Turning mad & wild drinking the nectar
from heaven gift of nature...
My wandering vision fully drenched
& drunk with the wine,
Searches the sea gulls for beautiful
blinking & storing in the mine,
The archives of the mine within the soul's fathomless vine,
The irresistible ambience was a sheer
magical creation of the divine,
Poets only imagine in ocean of the mind but the situation,
Happens somewhere else beyond the veil of infatuation,
The whispers of the soul vanished dreams in mixed fusion.

....

(409)

The Ire of the Hatred

When you strike the match stick,
Only fire will come out of the kick,
If you can't afford to tolerate the fire,
Better leave that place without any ire,
Hatred of the mind must not go express,
However you may try but can't suppress,
Somehow or rather the hatred wounds,
The wound behaves like a blood hound,
Taking a toll on life in profuse bleed,
The fire brigade fails to douse the fire,
Everything destroyed in minutes of the ire,
If it was meant for destruction let it,
Let it be destroyed why remember it,
Choice is yours can go to any extent,
There is no meaning with a false regret,
If the world does not know how to respect,
Let the world go its way leaving the arrest,
The world can't run with the arrest mindset,

When the calamity betrays resulting hurt,
Situations hounding with hunt by default,
The apple cart topples half-way with insult,
Nervous woes shivering veins feel the jolt,
The behavior comes scathing from the bolt,
Encounters of the assassination absurd fault,
Simplicity taken for a ride of the innocent,
When you strike the match stick,
Only fire will come out of the kick.

....

(410)

The Hive on my Window Sill

. . . .

A huge bee hive gives a feel,
Livelihood of honey bees on my window sill,
Honey makers eternally busy,
Without knowing the nectar stored in the sieve,
Nectar in the huge hive,
None dare go near the sieve,
Soldiers guarding the hive,
Tress-passers warned by nature,
The humming voice of the flies fear,
The honey bee an eternal fly of the nature,
Weaves the beautiful hives for a beautiful future,
A huge hive on my window sill,
Bathes me with freshness of incredible feel,
Un-harming honey bees round the clock stay busy,
Collecting tiny drops of honey from the flowers so easy,
Nectars of the sweet nature waters the mouth in such ease,
Oh! Wonderful Nature bowing at your creativity,
Singing the songs of eternity in tunes of infinity,
Scaring away the usual assassin,
A flying bird takes a bite from the stay,
The awakened soldiers chase them away,
A huge bee hive,
The soul takes a dive,
Dreams of life seen to thrive...

. . . .

(411)

Time & Again,

Caught in ire,
In the flash of the fire,
Destroy things in satire,
I do not know who set the fire,
Burning the castle into ashes,
In the ashes still breathes my existence,
The ashes flying with wind in silence,
Each particle of the ashes turning into invisible,
Invisible tiny dusts flying into sacred nature,
Nature's storehouse archives the dusts,
The soul of the ashes playing host,
The memory's huge archive,
Needs no testimony to describe,
The fear of the ghost hunts down,
Scared of the words fired frown,
The fear of the fire time & again,
Hurting sentiments of fried emotions,

(412)

The Scarlet Lover...

....

The scarlet lover,
Suffers from fever,
The rising temperature,
Water soaked plaster,
Missioning the fever,
Delirium state of the affair,
Undesired satire,
Calls to the doctor,
Yields no breather,
The pulse is the breaker,
Breaking beats into tear,
Jerked up tear from the eyes corner,
The helpless scarlet lover,
Dries up with a tissue paper,
Throwing the calamity in to gutter,
A silent prayer,
Come down Oh! Temperature,

Thou shall live forever,
Lying on the stretcher,
The helpless lover,
Crying for the loser,
The loser's painful tear,
Does not reach the ear,
Oh! God how to bear,
How to live without the lover,
The scarlet lover,

....

(413)

Never Atone...

Choice is yours,
As you choose,
So one chooses,
Much of our pain,
self-chosen,
Opportunity does not,
Show its face always,
The prerogative,
Can't be your sole choice,
Everything in this universe,
Have two sides,
When one falls,
The other too crumbles,
Time does not halt,
For a moment,
The invisible hand of time,
Keeps moving lest you trying,
Even if you do not sing,
The child will sleep crying,
How long can it cry?
In the end the cry will die,

All brothers do not have sisters,
All sisters do not have brothers,
Irony with the universe,
Life is a beautiful paradox,
In the paradigm you choose to live,
Others have their own choice to leave,
The universe is like that,
Full of satire false promises,
Tall promises to low assurances,
Never worry for what is gone,
Be gone &bye gone,
Forget the moment never atone,
Never atone for what you have not done,
Never again hope never again for ever again.

....

(414)

Quiet flows the Dawn..

Quiet flows the dawn,
Flowing in flamboyance reading then,
The universe is huge drama house of emotion,
None can surpass the human emotion,
No anger no annoyance in poetic motion,
Poets are loved worldwide,
The sea too welcomes the poet to its tides,
Sweet flows the dawn,
Travelling steps of life in the poetic lawn,
Incredible words sung,
Indelible words on the tongue,
Incredible words to hone,
Quiet flows the dawn,
The stream of poetry sail alone,
The reader in disguise feels lovelorn,
Accompanying the lone healing the pain,

(415)

The Journey just begins,

The oriental journey sailing across,
In a turbulent world of crisis,
The love songs will bring the nectar
of peace from the oasis,
The world will heave a sigh of relief,
For a brief moment the foundation of the soul,
Feel shaken by the poetical bell,
Ringing sublime words of tale,
Singing the rhyming words from the verse of the gale,
The poets of orient sweeping the soul's animosity,
Alliterations to metaphors in their soulful simplicity,
Carrying the poets of the orient together,
Singing lovely songs lovely beetles of the century,
Lovely symphonies of the sonata in harmony,
The Dense & deep woods,
Showing miles long hoods,
The mother in labour pains,
Waiting for the child to see the reigns,
Inheriting the autumnal leaves,
The wind breathes for a moment to live,
In each leaf a poet spreading his tentacles,
Epics of love in the pinnacles...

(416)

The Winking Dusk

....

Looks like the dusk winking,
From amidst the clouds hanger blinking,
The mind walks steps towards the horizon,
To catch a glimpse of the enlightened zone,
The vision takes a dip in the soul,
What the soul feels who can peel,
The west ward Sun,
Before sinking into the horizon,
Stepping into the hemisphere waiting in the western,
The night long journey ending with dawn,
The dawn marching in to the day with the radiant sun,
The stationary sun moving around the axis in rotation,
The picture of the winking dusk,
Spreading dust in the cloud's mask,
The lens man at times in an irresistible temptation,
Captivates the atmosphere inside the lens in vision,
To show case before his fans an impeccable fusion,
The great sequence of opulence of the horizon,
Creates a magic inside the soul's prison,

....

(417)

The Pyramid of Ego

Veins of ego,
Burn the soul's tango,
The soul ruminates,
For a while feel the pains,
The pains of being burnt,
The pain of the flames point,
The pains of pride & poise,
Flames eternally devour the truth,
The truth of the flames couth,
For little omissions what a price,
The omissions just taste spice,
Skeletal remains in the cupboard of time,
When one digs the skeleton of the ego,
Only skeletal remains of the mummies,
Mummies in the mortuaries,
Skeletons of the past centuries,
Hidden beneath the pyramid,
The pyramid of the ego,
Little realize the inside,
The skeletons of ego,
Hidden under the pyramid,
Veins of ego,
Burning the soul's tango.

(418)

Mysteries of the Memory lane

....

Down memory lane,
Mind visits like an insane,
The tiny thatched shed roof,
Memories of the moments proof,
Etched in the memories parlor,
The parlor recounts the valor,
The many evenings of our meeting,
The hands that caressed the painting,
Moving around the locks,
The long hair often falling over my face,
Under hairy duress the lips locking to kiss,
Breathing love packed sighs with hiss,
On the canvass of the soul we rolled,
Rocked in momentary moods boiled,
Boiling the bare truths of inventing tapestries,
The tapestries of the painted canvass,
Painting tattoos of love on my nude canvass,
The brush touched every point with kiss,
Painting the doves lovelorn bliss,

Love never ended remained unrequited forever,
The more of the invasions the more inquisitive fever,
Unravelling the inventing mind of never before done,
In engrossed silences we surrendered to one,
Carving a niche in the fountain of your soul,
Sailed too deep into the fathom of the gaol,
The down memory lane memories of the Taj Mahal,
Stands in monumental silence of the dome of marble,
Relics of the love stories written on the time's wall,

....

(419)

Oh! My Lord of the rings..

....

Feelings in the innocent tender grass of abundance,
In the droplets adoring the tender leaves in trance,
A budding tender flower in bloom,
The returning rains after a loaded downpour,
In the open winged birds symphonies,
In the purple red radiance of the afternoon,
Everywhere you,
The mundanely feelings cannot be felt,
Staying in the atoms of mine,
You,
Nestling in the soul's amber,
Hibernating in sub-conscious,
Unconsciously you resign to my sub-conscious,
Dreams of losing the little me,
The little me,
In dreams of being blessed with the eternal salvation,
From the cocoon of time till the fathom of vision,
Remain etched in my soul,
Oh! My lord of the rings do n't you feel,

....

(420)

The Innocent Rhymes

....

Caught you writing my name on the sands of time,
Surrendered with apology reading your innocent rhymes,
My birthday was just an alibi of the relentless mind,
Carving a niche for me you waited in mute silence to find,
You never wanted me know the gimmick of your surprises,
Always pricked holes in my tender
heart with soulful appraisals,
The birthday nearing the death day,
As long as you live leaving one birth day
after the other till the last day,
Can you assure me that you will wait
there for me till the final day?
If you wait will write your name on the sands of time,
Till time lasts the eternal lover will
write rhyme after rhyme.
Holding the invisible hands of time,

My fingers forming the symbol of love,
Will stand the testimony of time
scribbling rhymes in the grove,
When you behave like a dove,
Tweeting my names on your beaks trove,
I forget my own taking your name at the grove,
Let us not wait at the sands of time for love,
Engrave your name on my heart's enclosure,
Dreams of your passion becomes my treasure.

. . . .

(421)

The Dark Robes of the Night...

The dark robes of the night,
Leaving for the dawn to alight,
Holding the hand of the child,
The mother will lead as guide,
The light into the day to look bright,
The evening starts retiring to the night,
Sailing into the engrossed affair tight,
The fight ending into a passionate night,
Soothing solace for the soul to feel in flight,
Solace for soul just alight,
Soul starts reeling with slumber in sight,
Fairies of the dreamland slowly alight,
Each page of the dream pounding heart,
Wonderful dreams feel ecstatic,
The soul silently waking up from the static,
Brooding over the dreamland treasure emphatic,

The dark robes of night preparing to leave the night,
The dawn completing the nuptials before alight,
A bird of the dawn started practicing its usual song,
Practicing for hours before the dawn comes along,
The song of the dawn bird takes away the being,
In the flamboyant tunes harmony playing,
Playing a game of hide & seek since birth of time,
Singing round the clock the incessant rhyme,

Life lifelife the beautiful pantomime

....

(422)

Falling in Love

....

Eyes just hone beauty in perception of the mind's chapter,
Writing the small pores to the glistening
sweat drops with tear,
The aromatic fragrance of the lovers,
Attract each other madly to be in enclosure,
The aromatic fragrance smell pungent,
Body for the bodies to attract it is god sent,
Divinity in attraction of the pungency,
A mad attraction of seductive mind in insurgency,
In insurgent moods of flamboyance,
The mind fires its bullets through the eyes at the fiancé,
The fiancé falls into the lovelorn trap of the adolescence,
Writing havoc in dreamlands of the physics,
Attracting the opposite is an art of glamour,
Women wear the glamour for the men to adore,
Adoring the woman in life,
Man walks millions of miles into the galaxy of the cliff
The beloved's sweet dreams aromatic amber,
The long locks rolling down the posture,
The glamour of the beloved with antiquity of the jewelries,
Heals away the pains of the mind, body & soul
Of beloved to true cavalries,

Dreaming the beloved round the clock,
Breathing the impasse of the blocked
emotion in soul's truck,
The panting beloved lost in the
treasuries of dreaming the hack,
The fingers rolling down from tip to the toe,
Shivering with tickles the small pores of
physique drops the sweats to the glow,
The passionate moods love air tight embrace,
Digging the graves for bliss hood in soul's terrace,
The garden of soul blooming with flowers,
The flowers budding in to blooming towers,
Your ravishing looks just love,
You look so seductress beautiful,
As I stare at you I fall into your love...

....

(423)

The King of the Skies,

....

The ground below,
Looks hollow,
From altitude of the flight,
An immeasurable view of the depth,
Space's enigmatic domain,
No one here remain,
Clouds with the mist,
Sun beams feast,
Glances just travel the length,
Feelings of blankness toughest,
The parable of three Good Samaritan,
Strangers flying to one destination,
Glistening island of clouds,
The indigo with its wings flies abound,

Still the heaven is unfathomable,
Immeasurable,
From the depth of dense altitude,
Humans consuming time in galloping pace,
Opening its spread with pride invites of the space,
Traverse Oh! Man take care of me do not be harsh,
Always welcome to my vast dome,
As you wish I will wait at my home,
For a glimpse of your welcome....
Scribbled on my palms of altitude held in time...

....

(424)

The Galloping steps

Wonderful pace of the gallop,
Love the beautiful pace of the hilltop,
The painters' superb creativity,
Divine blessing to the humanity,
Staring with awe the humanity
Surrenders in mute reverence,
Inquisitive soul often faltering
At the meaning of existence,
The energetic pace in rhythmic sequence,
Feelings satiate the grieving mind with opulence,
Never surrender to the word defeat,
Just imagine the horse in galloping feat,
Life has mysteries hidden in its meanings never unravel,
Whole of life passes along the long pastures,
The past dreaming of future to marvel,
The enigmatic meaning of life a befitting sequel,
The gimmicks travel along,
Delving into the domain of solitude to belong,
The mysteries winking from the hideout,
Gallop the distance for meaningful event,
Wonderful space of the hilltop,
Love the pace of the steps of the gallop,

(425)

The Opulence of Space

Opulence of space,
Divinity at infinity's grace,
Mass of dense clouds,
Flamboyant dreams swimming in shroud,
Invisible to the human eye,
The soul ruminates feeling shy,
Dreams of my beloved,
To sail with the cloud,
From one end of the world,
To the other end,
Descending clouds come to defend,
Trust comes to ascend,
As we roll along the vast infinite space sail along,
Space exists in gaseous spheres,
Each sphere has its own gimmicks here,
Tunes blank choirs playing along,
Soul feels unfathomable of the belong,
The longings of the two souls,
Firing a match stick inside the soul,
The sparks engulfing the fuel,
Songs of eternity in the duel,

As we descend downward,
An invisible source from the seclusion pulling us upward,
Rolling & rocking in the heaven alighting downward,
The pressures fighting between themselves,
The secured boundaries not allowing the
pressures to push themselves,
Caught in between the outer & the inner pressures,
The child in unbearable pain crying in
the catapult of the pressures,
Tilting to sides the wings descend downward,
The long stretch of the green pastures
surrenders their ward...
Opulence of the galloping pace
Surrendering at divinity's grace,

....

(426)

Diffusion

When I am in distress,
Oh! Mom please,
Lessen my stress,
Just chant the name of yours,
Alight from nowhere,
Take my pain somewhere,
I just wonder at my existence,
How do you know my stance?
Even when you are not there,
In my telepathic communion here,
Reaches my message to you wherever you are,
My longing for you will end never,
Till death I seek you forever,
The complex universe,
The complex satire,
Take a toll on life without any reason,
Every moment here is such uncertain,

(427)

Autumn knocking at the Door...

Leaves leaving the trees,
Autumnal freebies,
The flowers on the pastures,
Dressing in the pink statures,
The nature adoring the season,
Street dogs engrossed in the game of copulation,
Mating with seductress in open,
The laws of creation its unknown meanings hidden,
Wonderfully crafted by the season,
The season giving feelings enliven,
Amazing purple spread of the dry leaves,
Giving feelings of ecstasy in lips,
Lips silently applying tip of the sticks,
Gearing up the moods for festive kicks,
Couples feeling blown in flamboyant moods,
Embracing with nature's purple woods,
On the shelter of the beloved's huge logs,
Feeling the heat of the beautiful blogs,
The huge logs in deep embrace,
Feelings of ecstasy in deep grace,
Breathing the autumnal solace,
The autumn in the middle of the year,
Mixed reactions mixed up passions in full gear,
The gear of the season taking full moon's day,
The huge moonlit radiance once in a year of the day,

The girls celebrate the month of October,
Offering prayers at the radiant full moon in the amber,
Beseeching blessings for the groom of their dreams,
Alight from destiny with colorful dreams in the realms,
A cake burnt whole of the night in wooden charcoal,
Mouth waters for a pie of the cake born from the fuel,
Girls wearing new looks sailing their
soul's in true happiness,
Before girlhood leaves the floors of adolescence,
The autumnal songs on the lips with essence,
Singing the season's humid weather in presence,
Men wearing the attire of ghosts,
Appear in the mid-night at the young
girls for the cake's taste,
The cake baked night long waits for the ghost,
The ghost is none other but a group of village youth,
Wearing a garb of straw & grass come in couth,
The festival celebrated throughout
Orissa as full moon night,
Radiance of moon lit radiance of the
shadows of the soul's in light,
Leafs leaving the trees spreading a purple red radiance,
The moods of nature in true regale
bashing with glory of the bash,

....

(428)

The Magic of Hope...

When time does not cope,
Never lose hope,
Time rekindles the lost hope,
The magic wand of time,
Gives one everything to rhyme,
From the layers of woes to sing the chime,
The layers of happiness sing the pantomime,
When time does not cope,
The magic wand of time rekindles hope,

(429)

Thirty long years of solitude

....

Thirty long years of solitude,
Why after leaving me at the altitude,
At least could have told my mistakes,
Murmurs in silence still bake,
Could not know where I was wrong,
What went such wrong?
Repudiated me to languish,
Thirty long years at the pass,
Still waiting for the glimpse of a glance,
The cruel saga of destiny writes the distance,
The cliff becomes friend of my existence,
The statue of my soul stands there in mute silence,
Lovers come to pray put a wreath at the monument,
Inside the roaring sea stands the lover's point,
The roaring sea tells the saga of the soul,
Even striking against the solid rock does not heal,
Promising me never to return to the point,
Left in huff with a swollen face of the anoint,

Paying wreathe in your memory life long,
One hundred year' s of solitude will be too long,
Difficult for time to wait that long,
Better if understanding comes come along,
Promise never to leave the point,
Whether life is there or not keep
waiting at the immortal joint...
Even thirty years pass in between,
Promise to wait hundreds of years in between.

....

(430)

THE SILENCE KILLS...

. . . .

The silence kills,
The response heals,
Knowing pretty well,
Just she dwells,
Dwelling in her domain,
In solitude she remains,
Little response please,
Little understanding of ease,
But when calamity befall,
She still does not call,
The expected call dies in the soul,
No one understands the situation,
Cursing the tides for the mad infatuation,
A place in your soul,
Could have saved my sail,
Anchoring at the shore,
Could have sailed ashore,

But tantrums of yours,
Simply invincible like towers,
The inferno already in,
Flames spreading in,
Can't save existence,
Despite best of stance,
The silence kills,
Little response heals...

....

(431)

THE LAST LAUGH...

....

The last leaf that falls laughing from
the trees of September,
Feels the ambience with one more
leaf on the yard of amber,
The amber with a whiff of the wind moves the leafs to life,
The dry lifeless leafs just breathing happiness in true rife,
Until the last laugh leaves the mouth of the season,
The season breathes in silence with a reason,
Murmuring to itself traces of the last laugh with treason,
Eaten into the galloping pace of the autumnal banter,
The season just heaves a sigh of
relief soliciting the October,
What happened in the heart of September
before its last breathe,
Shadows of September takes umbrage
honored the in wreathe,
The smiling face of September with
the dry leafs of the yard,
September bids goodbye to the last
days of the truth said hard...
The last laugh etched in memoriam
in the times' graveyard,

....

(432)

Uncle Rashid of the Childhood...

....

Mouthwatering dishes,
Tongue feeling the delicious,
Childhood looks as if it was yesterday,
A feast of the delicious sweet dish,
One Muslim uncle in our neighborhood,
Uncle Rashid loved the children of the colony being fed,
Come happy Eid,
Come Ramjan,
Come Muharram,
They prepared the dry fruits to the awesome sweet dishes,
Spreading the festive moods with fragrance,
Our infant whims dreamt of the delicacies,
Just yesterday expressed to a Muslim friend,
Can you please invite me for a taste of the sweet dish?
The child in me was feeling a backlash,
Visiting again the same lanes
For taste of the mouth-watering dish,
Uncle Rashid is gone to heaven long back,
But memories do not leave the lost track,

Once again once again
Oh! God if you could roll back,
Roll back time to Uncle Rashid's home
For re-amassing the lost threads lying there,
A tribute of soul memorizing the tracks here,
Uncle Rashid where ever you be,
Rest in peace, peace there be,
A pious man of beads in hands chanting the rhyme,
Praying round the clock sublime
With you the bond will remain long,
A childhood dream dreamt life long,

....

(433)

The Silent Monk...

....

The Monastery stood like a silent monk,
Waiting for the divine for the world to bunk,
Thousand lights,
Lamps in honor,
Wheels of scripture,
On the rotor,
Thousand prayers,
Little dude monks,
Garbed in orange flank,
Tiptoed from the neck,
The attire of renounce,
Silent prayers in announce,
The Rumbek monastery,
Buddhist hymns chanted in mastery,
A humming voice as if chanting Mom,
Resounding with the echoes of walled dome,
When my soul alighted from me,
Could never pulse the real me,
Lost in the silence of the thousand lamps,
Lighting with radiance the huge hall of lamps,
The whining little monks playing a sweet
music from the mouthorgan,

The prayer song play backed to soothe the human,
The dome of peace with fortunes of the divine grace,
All souls lost with mesmeric ambience in sheer bliss,
The innocent drooping eyes of the Tibetan lama brethren,
Child to adult all in one unique transcendence of heaven,
The Hills with its cunning peaks & the cleavages,
Gave a picturesque view of highest Himalayan ranges,
Fired glances just travelled the distance long as much,
Never feeling tired of the glistening
snow clad mountains as such,
Thousand lights,
Thousand prayers,
Wheels of scriptures,
On the rotor,

....

The famous Rumtek Monastery is
in Gangtok, Sikkim, India.

(434)

Bye September bye

Bye September bye,
Bowing with a shy,
Leaving the amber fast,
The Dye is cast,
Today you leave,
Tomorrow we live,
Life is eternal,
Even though ephemeral,
The truth such cardinal,
Whoever comes on the rotation?
Leave one day with a short notation,
Rhyming the notation we live,
Rhyming the notation we believe,
Bye September bye,
Before tomorrow arrives bowing with a shy,
Memories of you hunt for time,
Memoirs written on the sands in rhyme,
Bye September bye,
Dry leafs mourn the absence feeling shy,
Even today is the last day we do not cry,
Waiting for your arrival until the next pie,

(435)

One meet of the eyes

With one meet of the eye,
She smiled with a shy,
Extempore infatuation,
Desire of soul in ambition,
One meeting in culmination,
The dreams of then,
Not ending the sequence chain,
Waiting at the point,
Where the eyes met,
For a glimpse of the smile,
By default the Achilles heel,
The cupid's attraction,
A divine sanction,
With one meet of the glance,
Sending me signals to trance,
Giggling at my predicament,
Calling me a fool of lovers net,
The lover roping in duress,
Her flamboyant smiles in opulence,

Pumping life into my bone,
My bones of love feeling the boon,
God sent messages of the eyes,
Soul boiling for embrace in fries,
The beloved slowly walks in,
To the point of no return with fin,
Inside the aquarium of the universe,
Sailing like pair of glistening fish,
Every moment touching,
Every moment pricking,
Kiss, love & swim,
In moods & whims,
The fragile sense of the soul,
Attracting the beloved to magic bowl....

....

(436)

Reader's please Digest...

For my Readers with love,
My anxious soul in ransom for your love,
If you could rate them,
My poetic soul will humble them,
Your feedback is my food for thought,
Holding you in high esteem forever must,
May the world learn more?
Knowledge is true faith & true power.
Knowledge will unravel more & more,
Bowing with reverence,
Will you comment on my flamboyance?
The Universe is huge place,
Space of the Universe still feels less,
Let love flow with abundance,
Let the pains of the world convert to pleasure in opulence,
Prayer before Almighty,
Peace must live till Eternity.
Peace must prevail till Infinity.
Human Faith must remain in Unity.
Standing Ovation to friends, relatives,
family & the Poetic Fraternity.
May the Dew Drops sing the poems of eternity?

END

Review of my Book "THE DEW DROPS" by Poet Damodar Boruah

Author Whispering Windows Published by Patridge India

REVIEW

A WORDSWORTH SHELTERS IN HIM!

Why poems are composed? There are different opinions-some share views, for some passion of expressing different sagas of life as life is a lesson for them and for some-poetry is just resorting to therapy. In case of Akshaya Kumar Das's case, Manager in United India Insurance Co Ltd, a resident of Orissa, has a passion of unfolding his arduous journey of rags-to-riches with the rich tapestry of melodies and woes of contemporary time.

Akshaya's epic sized latest anthology 'The Dew Drops..."-collection of 436 poems composed in the period of 2014 and 2015 published by Partridge India Ltd, A Penguin Random House Company, makes a foray into the realm of English literature. The distinction he has achieved today among literary luminaries is the result of shortcomings of a life or tragedies caused by humanity and the imagination of an ordinary emotional man like him- has converted those ruminating thoughts into delighting pen into various poetry mainly in 'free verse', 'aabb' and 'occassional' style.

The deep reverence to Dr.APJ Abdul Kalam, Hon'ble President Of India in 'Tribute To A True Hero...', enlightening Buddha, sketching Konark Temple, delighting Durga Puja, colorful Christmas celebration are showcased colorfully reminding rich history, unity in diversity, exotic locations, preparation for a developed nation citizenship and so forth thereby uplifting the image of 'Incredible India' to aspiring domestic and international tourists.

His entire poem profile myriads of subjects from enthralling school poem- 'Mickey Mouse..' to scientific 'The Alien Universe...', importance of Father's day to urgency of International Day of Yoga, inclusion of poem on the eve of Poesis Award for seven poets, featuring of a selected poem in 'A Divine Madness' published by Ardus Publication, devastation of the Monument Dharara of Nepal, global warming, love and so many. Akshaya's brilliant 'Daffodils' takes one sensuously to perceive the line of Wordsworth's famous poem 'Daffodils': Beside the lake, beneath the trees,/ Fluttering and Dancing in the breeze. The genius in him is showed in 'The Village School..' and 'The poem ending with the 'N'!

A poem without emotion can't be considered a good poem. Akshaya displays a vivid description of a woman with warring-mind who wants to commit suicide from a cliff but the fetus how it pleads with the mother not to take such heinous attempt in 'Standing On The Cliff Of A Life':' the foetus calling in frantic pain/dissuading the negative mind/ Oh! Mom please be kind/Let me see the light/I'll stand by your side. The dexterity of using words creating image and experience in 'The Banyan grace...' delights a visual feast to any reader far on board amidst of the a sea as though one would enjoy the tree standing on the shore enjoying the swift breeze.

The remarkable achievement of Akshaya's poetry is in his stark simplicity, spontaneity, skill in using characters and appealing application of metaphors, similes, alliteration, onomatopoeia delineating the originality, maturity of his craftsmanship. The 'title' draws much attention of the readers but it's less visible in some of his poems just to hook the readers at the first glimpse in spite of all each of his poems looks entertaining, enlightening, rejuvenating for the body of the poem soaks curiosity to read and reap its meaning hence the anthology is successful and drawing immense hope among literary fraternity all over the world.

Akshaya Kumar Das has once again set an icon that the background of different profession is able to reach and shelter in the hearts of the elementary school children, scientists, scholars even the fresher's with the magic of rhymes and rhythms. It's the proud moment for Indian subcontinent a fertile mind which hitherto has not been recognized, now he is recognized with "The Dew Drops..."-a Wordsworth shelters in him, all must preserve him!

Poet Damodar Boruah, Guwahati, Assam
Author "Whispering Windows"

Review by Dr. Madhuchhanda Patra, Reader in English, Bhubaneswar on my book "THE DEW DROPS"

REVIEW

Sri Akshaya Kumar Das as a Poet seems to be working on a secret strategy to endow the poetic form with new dimension that represents the complexities of life. The Omniscient gaze of the Poet moves from the mother's womb to the "take world" of pain and the life's 'daily' reveals the 'COST OF EXISTENCE' where there is nothing to eat 'ONLY LOVE IS EATEN', where the "rose bud only patches up the differences, between warring minds to nations". The Poet here sets up his journey in the curvy path of life. The Path is more or less like the two roads of Robert Frost; one trodden and the other not being trodden instigates the poet to explore its mysteriousness and that makes all the difference. Here Mr.Das gropes in the 'innocent blackness' of creativity and at times dwells in the puzzles of existence. In 'the Domain of silent words' the expression of the poet through 'Silent Words' becomes bold and makes the departure more horrifying.

The Poet's mind is like an autumn tree that sheds its thoughts to create a space for the new. He has a mind that shines in emptiness; when the thoughts evaporate they condense sometimes to shower the world with visionary depths.

Sri Das is both a nature and realistic Poet. His Visionary depths not only measures the pains of existence but also beauties of rose and lotus. While walking on the thorns of life he cannot help looking at "the lotus goes blooming, the eyes fixed over the beauty smiling".

His Poem 'The Palpable Kick' flows with simple lucid style revealing the Poet's romantic confidence. But the romantic attitude is never an obstruction in his observation of haves and have nots where the 'haves lack the basic value of life, forget about the havenot's who are bereft of thing'.

The Beauty of rose and lotus has never taken the poet away from the world of reality, the world of truth. He has realized that the truth is absolute feelings for self….for the soul's selves to enlightenment….When the real world with distorted visions through smokes, destroying the eco system, whereas man betrays man, the visible hands openly betray; the poet finds solace in those invisible hands of God that always protects.

The Poet's Journey from Nature and Reality to Spirituality is definitely awesome sauce.

[Dr.Madhuchhanda Patra]
Reader in English,
Bhubaneswar, Orissa, India.

Printed in the United States
By Bookmasters